Old-Fashioned
Bake Sale

Laurie
Korsgaden
Watercolors

pil

Publications International, Ltd.
Favorite Brand Name Recipes at www.fbnr.com

Illustrated by Laurie Korsgaden © 2003.

Pictured on the back cover *(top to bottom):* Peanut Butter Mini Muffins *(page 128)* and Chocolatey Raspberry Crumb Bars *(page 60).*

ISBN: 0-7853-9295-5

Library of Congress Control Number: 2003101565

Manufactured in China.

8 7 6 5 4 3 2 1

Microwave Cooking: Microwave ovens vary in wattage. Use the cooking times as guidelines and check for doneness before adding more time.

Preparation/Cooking Times: Preparation times are based on the approximate amount of time required to assemble the recipe before cooking, baking, chilling or serving. These times include preparation steps such as measuring, chopping and mixing. The fact that some preparations and cooking can be done simultaneously is taken into account. Preparation of optional ingredients and serving suggestions is not included.

Contents

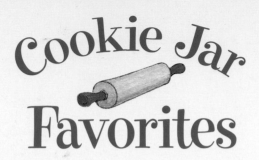

Cookie Jar Favorites

Oatmeal Toffee Cookies

- 1 cup (2 sticks) butter or margarine, softened
- 2 eggs
- 2 cups packed light brown sugar
- 2 teaspoons vanilla extract
- 1¾ cups all-purpose flour
- 1 teaspoon baking soda
- 1 teaspoon ground cinnamon
- ½ teaspoon salt
- 3 cups quick-cooking oats
- 1¾ cups (10-ounce package) HEATH® Almond Toffee Bits or SKOR® English Toffee Bits
- 1 cup MOUNDS® Coconut Flakes (optional)

1. Heat oven to 375°F. Lightly grease cookie sheet. Beat butter, eggs, brown sugar and vanilla until well blended. Add flour, baking soda, cinnamon and salt; beat until blended. Stir in oats, toffee and coconut, if desired, with spoon. Drop dough by rounded teaspoons about 2 inches apart onto prepared sheet.

2. Bake 8 to 10 minutes or until edges are lightly browned. Cool 1 minute; remove to wire rack.

Makes about 4 dozen cookies

Mini Chip Snowball Cookies

1½ cups (3 sticks) butter or margarine, softened

¾ cup powdered sugar

1 tablespoon vanilla extract

½ teaspoon salt

3 cups all-purpose flour

2 cups (12-ounce package) NESTLÉ® TOLL
   HOUSE® Semi-Sweet Chocolate Mini Morsels

½ cup finely chopped nuts

Powdered sugar

PREHEAT oven to 375°F.

BEAT butter, sugar, vanilla extract and salt in large mixer bowl until creamy. Gradually beat in flour; stir in morsels and nuts. Shape level tablespoons of dough into 1¼-inch balls. Place on ungreased baking sheets.

BAKE for 10 to 12 minutes or until cookies are set and lightly browned. Remove from oven. Sift powdered sugar over hot cookies on baking sheets. Cool on baking sheets for 10 minutes; remove to wire racks to cool completely. Sprinkle with additional powdered sugar, if desired. Store in airtight containers.   *Makes about 5 dozen cookies*

Mini Chip
Snowball Cookies

Cinnamon Roll Cookies

Cinnamon Mixture
> 4 tablespoons granulated sugar
> 1 tablespoon ground cinnamon

Cookie Dough
> 1 Butter Flavor CRISCO® Stick or 1 cup Butter Flavor CRISCO® all-vegetable shortening
> 1 cup firmly packed light brown sugar
> 2 large eggs
> 1 teaspoon vanilla
> 3 cups all-purpose flour
> 2 teaspoons baking powder
> ½ teaspoon salt
> 1 teaspoon ground cinnamon

1. For cinnamon mixture, combine granulated sugar and 1 tablespoon cinnamon in small bowl; mix well. Set aside.

2. For cookie dough, combine shortening and brown sugar in large bowl. Beat at medium speed with electric mixer until well blended. Beat in eggs and vanilla until well blended.

3. Combine flour, baking powder, salt and 1 teaspoon cinnamon in small bowl. Add to creamed mixture; mix well.

4. Turn dough onto sheet of waxed paper. Spread into 9×6-inch rectangle using rubber spatula. Sprinkle with 4 tablespoons cinnamon mixture to within 1 inch of edge.

continued on page 10

Cinnamon Roll Cookies

Cinnamon Roll Cookies, *continued*

Slowly roll up jelly-roll style into log. (If dough cracks, smooth with fingers while rolling.) Dust log with remaining cinnamon mixture. Wrap tightly in plastic wrap; refrigerate 4 hours or overnight.

5. Heat oven to 375°F. Spray cookie sheets with CRISCO® No-Stick Cooking Spray.

6. Slice dough ¼ inch thick. Place on prepared cookie sheets. Bake at 350°F for 8 minutes or until lightly browned on top. Cool on cookie sheets 4 minutes; transfer to cooling racks.   *Makes about 5 dozen cookies*

Three-in-One Chocolate Chip Cookies

6 tablespoons butter or margarine, softened
½ cup packed light brown sugar
¼ cup granulated sugar
1 egg
1 teaspoon vanilla extract
1½ cups all-purpose flour
½ teaspoon baking soda
¼ teaspoon salt
2 cups (12-ounce package) HERSHEY'S Semi-Sweet Chocolate Chips

Beat butter, brown sugar and granulated sugar in large bowl until fluffy. Add egg and vanilla; beat well. Stir together flour, baking soda and salt; gradually blend into butter mixture. Stir in chocolate chips. Shape and bake cookies into one of the three versions that follow.

Giant Cookie: Prepare dough. Heat oven to 350°F. Line 12×⅝-inch round pizza pan with foil. Pat dough evenly into prepared pan to within ¾ inch of edge. Bake 15 to 18 minutes or until lightly browned. Cool completely; cut into wedges. Decorate or garnish as desired. Makes about 8 servings (one 12-inch cookie).

Medium-Size Refrigerator Cookies: Prepare dough. On wax paper, shape into 2 rolls, 1½ inches in diameter. Wrap in wax paper; cover with plastic wrap. Refrigerate several hours, or until firm enough to slice. Heat oven to 350°F. Remove rolls from refrigerator; remove wrapping. With sharp knife, cut into ¼-inch-wide slices. Place on ungreased cookie sheet, about 3 inches apart. Bake 8 to 10 minutes or until lightly browned. Cool slightly; remove from cookie sheet to wire rack. Cool completely. Makes about 2½ dozen (2½-inch) cookies.

Miniature Cookies: Prepare dough. Heat oven to 350°F. Drop dough by ¼ teaspoons onto ungreased cookie sheet, about 1½ inches apart. (Or, spoon dough into disposable plastic frosting bag; cut about ¼ inch off tip. Squeeze batter by ¼ teaspoons onto ungreased cookie sheet.) Bake 5 to 7 minutes or just until set. Cool slightly; remove from cookie sheet to wire rack. Cool completely. Makes about 18½ dozen (¾-inch) cookies.

Cookie Pizza

1 (18-ounce) package refrigerated sugar cookie
   dough
2 cups (12 ounces) semi-sweet chocolate chips
1 (14-ounce) can EAGLE® BRAND Sweetened
   Condensed Milk (NOT evaporated milk)
2 cups candy-coated milk chocolate candies
2 cups miniature marshmallows
½ cup peanuts

1. Preheat oven 375°F. Press cookie dough into
2 ungreased 12-inch pizza pans. Bake 10 minutes or
until golden. Remove from oven.

2. In medium-sized saucepan, melt chips with Eagle
Brand. Spread over crusts. Sprinkle with milk chocolate
candies, marshmallows and peanuts.

3. Bake 4 minutes or until marshmallows are lightly
toasted. Cool. Cut into wedges.

Makes 2 pizzas (24 servings)

Prep Time: 15 minutes
Bake Time: 14 minutes

Cookie Pizza

Dino-Mite Dinosaurs

1 cup (2 sticks) butter, softened
1¼ cups granulated sugar
1 large egg
2 squares (1 ounce each) semi-sweet chocolate, melted
½ teaspoon vanilla extract
2⅓ cups all-purpose flour
1 teaspoon baking powder
¼ teaspoon salt
1 cup white frosting
Assorted food colorings
1 cup "M&M's"® Chocolate Mini Baking Bits

In large bowl cream butter and sugar until light and fluffy; beat in egg, chocolate and vanilla. In medium bowl combine flour, baking powder and salt; add to creamed mixture. Wrap and refrigerate dough 2 to 3 hours. Preheat oven to 350°F. Working with half the dough at a time on lightly floured surface, roll to ¼-inch thickness. Cut into dinosaur shapes using 4-inch cookie cutters. Place about 2 inches apart on ungreased cookie sheets. Bake 10 to 12 minutes. Cool 2 minutes on cookie sheets; cool completely on wire racks. Tint frosting desired colors. Frost cookies and decorate with "M&M's"® Chocolate Mini Baking Bits. Store in tightly covered container.

Makes 2 dozen cookies

Dino-Mite Dinosaurs

Chocolate Malted Cookies

¾ cup firmly packed light brown sugar

⅔ CRISCO® Stick or ⅔ cup CRISCO all-vegetable shortening

1 teaspoon vanilla

1 egg

1¾ cups all-purpose flour

½ cup malted milk powder

⅓ cup unsweetened cocoa powder

¾ teaspoon baking soda

½ teaspoon salt

2 cups malted milk balls, broken into large pieces*

*Place malted milk balls in heavy resealable plastic bag; break malted milk balls with rolling pin or back of heavy spoon.

1. Heat oven to 375°F. Place sheets of foil on countertop for cooling cookies.

2. Place brown sugar, shortening and vanilla in large bowl. Beat at medium speed of electric mixer until well blended. Add egg; beat well.

3. Combine flour, malted milk powder, cocoa, baking soda and salt. Add to shortening mixture; beat at low speed just until blended. Stir in malted milk pieces.

4. Drop dough by rounded measuring tablespoonfuls 2 inches apart onto ungreased baking sheets.

5. Bake one baking sheet at a time at 375°F for 7 to 9 minutes or until cookies are set. *Do not overbake*. Cool 2 minutes on baking sheets. Remove cookies to foil. *Makes about 3 dozen cookies*

Jumbo 3-Chip Cookies

4 cups all-purpose flour

1 teaspoon baking powder

1 teaspoon baking soda

1½ cups (3 sticks) butter, softened

1¼ cups granulated sugar

1¼ cups packed brown sugar

2 large eggs

1 tablespoon vanilla extract

1 cup (6 ounces) NESTLÉ® TOLL HOUSE®
   Milk Chocolate Morsels

1 cup (6 ounces) NESTLÉ® TOLL HOUSE®
   Semi-Sweet Chocolate Morsels

½ cup NESTLÉ® TOLL HOUSE® Premier
   White Morsels

1 cup chopped nuts

PREHEAT oven to 375°F.

COMBINE flour, baking powder and baking soda in medium bowl. Beat butter, granulated sugar and brown sugar in large mixer bowl until creamy. Beat in eggs and vanilla extract. Gradually beat in flour mixture. Stir in morsels and nuts. Drop dough by level ¼-cup measure 2 inches apart onto ungreased baking sheets.

BAKE for 12 to 14 minutes or until light golden brown. Cool on baking sheets for 2 minutes; remove to wire racks to cool completely.   *Makes about 2 dozen cookies*

Toffee Chunk Brownie Cookies

1 cup (2 sticks) butter
4 ounces unsweetened chocolate, coarsely chopped
1½ cups sugar
2 eggs
1 tablespoon vanilla
3 cups all-purpose flour
⅛ teaspoon salt
1½ cups coarsely chopped chocolate-covered
   toffee bars

Preheat oven to 350°F. Melt butter and chocolate in large saucepan over low heat, stirring until smooth. Remove from heat; cool slightly.

Stir sugar into chocolate mixture until smooth. Stir in eggs until well blended. Stir in vanilla until smooth. Stir in flour and salt just until mixed. Fold in chopped toffee bars.

Drop heaping tablespoonfuls of dough 1½ inches apart onto ungreased cookie sheets.

Bake 12 minutes or until just set. Let cookies stand on cookie sheets 5 minutes; transfer to wire racks to cool completely. Store in airtight container.

Makes 36 cookies

**Toffee Chunk
Brownie Cookies**

Peanut Butter and Jelly Cookies

1 Butter Flavor CRISCO® Stick or 1 cup Butter
  Flavor CRISCO® all-vegetable shortening
1 cup JIF® Creamy Peanut Butter
1 teaspoon vanilla
⅔ cup firmly packed light brown sugar
⅓ cup granulated sugar
2 large eggs
2 cups all-purpose flour
1 cup SMUCKER'S® Strawberry Preserves
  or any flavor

1. Heat oven to 350°F. Combine shortening, peanut butter and vanilla in food processor fitted with metal blade. Process until well blended and smooth. Add sugars; process until incorporated completely. Add eggs; beat just until blended. Add flour; pulse until dough begins to form ball. *Do not overprocess.*

2. Place dough in medium bowl. Shape ½ tablespoon dough into ball for each cookie. Place 1½ inches apart on ungreased cookie sheets. Press thumb into center of each ball to create deep well. Fill each well with about ½ teaspoon preserves.

3. Bake at 350°F for 10 minutes or until lightly browned and firm. Cool on cookie sheets 4 minutes; transfer to cooling racks. Leave on racks about 30 minutes or until completely cool.   *Makes about 5 dozen cookies*

Peanut Butter and
Jelly Cookies

Original Nestlé® Toll House® Chocolate Chip Cookies

2¼ cups all-purpose flour

1 teaspoon baking soda

1 teaspoon salt

1 cup (2 sticks) butter or margarine, softened

¾ cup granulated sugar

¾ cup packed brown sugar

1 teaspoon vanilla extract

2 large eggs

2 cups (12-ounce package) NESTLÉ® TOLL HOUSE® Semi-Sweet Chocolate Morsels

1 cup chopped nuts

PREHEAT oven to 375°F.

COMBINE flour, baking soda and salt in small bowl. Beat butter, granulated sugar, brown sugar and vanilla extract in large mixer bowl until creamy. Add eggs, one at a time, beating well after each addition. Gradually beat in flour mixture. Stir in morsels and nuts. Drop by rounded tablespoon onto ungreased baking sheets.

BAKE for 9 to 11 minutes or until golden brown. Cool on baking sheets for 2 minutes; remove to wire racks to cool completely.   *Makes about 5 dozen cookies*

Original Nestlé® Toll House®
Chocolate Chip Cookies

Chocolate Peanut Butter Chip Cookies

8 (1-ounce) squares semi-sweet chocolate

3 tablespoons butter or margarine

1 (14-ounce) can EAGLE® BRAND Sweetened Condensed Milk (NOT evaporated milk)

2 cups biscuit baking mix

1 egg

1 teaspoon vanilla extract

1 cup (6 ounces) peanut butter-flavored chips

1. Preheat oven to 350°F. In large saucepan over low heat, melt chocolate and butter with Eagle Brand; remove from heat. Add biscuit mix, egg and vanilla; with mixer, beat until smooth and well blended.

2. Let mixture cool to room temperature. Stir in peanut butter chips. Shape into 1¼-inch balls. Place 2 inches apart on ungreased baking sheets. Bake 6 to 8 minutes or until tops are lightly crusty. Cool. Store tightly covered at room temperature.   *Makes about 4 dozen cookies*

Prep Time: 15 minutes
Bake Time: 6 to 8 minutes

Chewy Oatmeal Cookies

¾ Butter Flavor CRISCO® Stick or ¾ cup Butter
   Flavor CRISCO® all-vegetable shortening
   plus additional for greasing
1¼ cups firmly packed light brown sugar
1 egg
⅓ cup milk
1½ teaspoons vanilla
3 cups quick oats, uncooked
1 cup all-purpose flour
½ teaspoon baking soda
½ teaspoon salt
¼ teaspoon ground cinnamon
1 cup raisins
1 cup coarsely chopped walnuts

1. Heat oven to 375°F. Grease baking sheets with shortening. Place sheets of foil on countertop for cooling cookies.

2. Combine ¾ cup shortening, brown sugar, egg, milk and vanilla in large bowl. Beat at medium speed of electric mixer until well blended.

3. Combine oats, flour, baking soda, salt and cinnamon. Mix into creamed mixture at low speed just until blended. Stir in raisins and nuts.

4. Drop rounded tablespoonfuls of dough 2 inches apart onto prepared baking sheet.

5. Bake one baking sheet at a time at 375°F for 10 to 12 minutes, or until lightly browned. *Do not overbake.* Cool 2 minutes on baking sheet. Remove cookies to foil to cool completely.   *Makes about 2½ dozen cookies*

Crispy's Irresistible Peanut Butter Marbles

1 package (18 ounces) refrigerated peanut butter cookie dough

2 cups "M&M's"® Milk Chocolate Mini Baking Bits, divided

1 cup crisp rice cereal, divided (optional)

1 package (18 ounces) refrigerated sugar cookie dough

¼ cup unsweetened cocoa powder

In large bowl combine peanut butter dough, 1 cup "M&M's"® Milk Chocolate Mini Baking Bits and ½ cup cereal, if desired. Remove dough to small bowl; set aside. In large bowl combine sugar dough and cocoa powder until well blended. Stir in remaining 1 cup "M&M's"® Milk Chocolate Mini Baking Bits and remaining ½ cup cereal, if desired. Remove half the dough to small bowl; set aside. Combine half the peanut butter dough with half the chocolate dough by folding together just enough to marble. Shape marbled dough into 8×2-inch log. Wrap log in plastic wrap. Repeat with remaining doughs. Refrigerate logs 2 hours. To bake, preheat oven to 350°F. Cut dough into ¼-inch-thick slices. Place about 2 inches apart on ungreased cookie sheets. Bake 12 to 14 minutes. Cool 1 minute on cookie sheets; cool completely on wire racks. Store in tightly covered container.

Makes 5 dozen cookies

Crispy's Irresistible Peanut Butter Marbles

Black & White Hearts

¾ cup sugar

1 cup butter, softened

1 package (3 ounces) cream cheese, softened

1 egg

1½ teaspoons vanilla

3 cups all-purpose flour

1 cup semisweet chocolate chips

2 tablespoons shortening

1. Combine sugar, butter, cream cheese, egg and vanilla in large bowl. Beat at medium speed of electric mixer, scraping bowl often, until light and fluffy. Add flour; beat until well mixed. Divide dough in half; wrap each half in waxed paper. Refrigerate 2 hours or until firm.

2. Preheat oven to 375°F. Roll out dough to ⅛-inch thickness on lightly floured surface. Cut out with lightly floured 2-inch heart-shaped cookie cutter. Place 1 inch apart on ungreased cookie sheets. Bake 7 to 10 minutes or until edges are very lightly browned. Remove immediately to wire racks to cool completely.

3. Melt chocolate chips and shortening in small saucepan over low heat 4 to 6 minutes or until melted. Dip half of each heart into melted chocolate. Refrigerate on cookie sheets or trays lined with waxed paper until chocolate is firm. Store, covered, in refrigerator.

Makes about 3½ dozen

Black & White Hearts

Chocolate-Coconut-Toffee Delights

½ cup all-purpose flour
¼ teaspoon baking powder
¼ teaspoon salt
1 package (12 ounces) semisweet chocolate chips, divided
¼ cup butter, cut into small pieces
¾ cup packed light brown sugar
2 eggs, beaten
1 teaspoon vanilla
1½ cups flaked coconut
1 cup toffee baking pieces

1. Preheat oven to 350°F. Line cookie sheets with parchment paper.

2. Combine flour, baking powder and salt in small bowl; set aside. Place 1 cup chocolate chips in large microwavable bowl. Microwave at HIGH 1 minute; stir. Microwave 30 to 60 seconds more or until chips are melted; stir well.

3. Add butter to bowl; stir until melted. Beat in brown sugar, eggs and vanilla until well blended. Beat in flour mixture until blended. Stir in coconut, toffee pieces and remaining 1 cup chocolate chips.

4. Drop dough by heaping ⅓ cupfuls onto prepared cookie sheets, spacing 3 inches apart. Flatten with rubber spatula into 3½-inch circles. Bake 15 to 17 minutes or until edges are just firm to the touch. Cool cookies on cookie sheets 2 minutes; slide parchment paper and cookies onto countertop. Cool completely.

Makes 1 dozen (5-inch) cookies

Lemon Cookies

1 package DUNCAN HINES® Moist Deluxe®
    Lemon Supreme Cake Mix
2 eggs
⅓ cup vegetable oil
1 tablespoon lemon juice
¾ cup chopped nuts or flaked coconut
    Confectioners' sugar

1. Preheat oven to 375°F. Grease baking sheets.

2. Combine cake mix, eggs, oil and lemon juice in large bowl. Beat at low speed with electric mixer until well blended. Add nuts. Shape dough into 1-inch balls. Place 1 inch apart on prepared baking sheets.

3. Bake at 375°F for 6 to 7 minutes or until lightly browned. Cool 1 minute on baking sheets. Remove to cooling racks. Sprinkle with confectioners' sugar.

Makes about 3 dozen cookies

Tip: You can frost cookies with 1 cup confectioners' sugar mixed with 1 tablespoon lemon juice instead of sprinkling cookies with confectioners' sugar.

Sun Dried Cranberry-Walnut Oatmeal Cookies

¾ Butter Flavor CRISCO® Stick or ¾ cup Butter
    Flavor CRISCO® all-vegetable shortening
¾ cup granulated sugar
¾ cup firmly packed light brown sugar
2 large eggs
1 teaspoon vanilla
1 cup all-purpose flour
1 teaspoon baking soda
¼ teaspoon salt
2¾ cups rolled oats
1 cup sun dried cranberries
1 cup walnut pieces

1. Heat oven to 375°F.

2. Combine shortening and sugars in large bowl. Beat
at medium speed with electric mixer until well blended.
Beat in eggs and vanilla until well blended.

3. Combine flour, baking soda and salt in small bowl.
Stir into creamed mixture; mix well. Add oats, sun
dried cranberries and walnuts. Spray cookie sheets with
CRISCO® No-Stick Cooking Spray. Dust with flour. Drop
dough by teaspoonfuls about 2 inches apart onto prepared
cookie sheets. Bake at 375°F for 8 minutes or until firm
and brown. Cool on cookie sheets 4 minutes; transfer to
cooling rack.   *Makes about 6 dozen cookies*

Sun Dried Cranberry-
Walnut Oatmeal Cookies

Chocolate Peanut Butter Cup Cookies

Cookies

> 1 cup semisweet chocolate chips
>
> 2 squares (1 ounce each) unsweetened baking chocolate
>
> 1 cup sugar
>
> ½ Butter Flavor CRISCO® Stick or ½ cup Butter Flavor CRISCO® all-vegetable shortening
>
> 2 eggs
>
> 1 teaspoon salt
>
> 1 teaspoon vanilla
>
> 1½ cups plus 2 tablespoons all-purpose flour
>
> ½ teaspoon baking soda
>
> ¾ cup finely chopped peanuts
>
> 36 miniature peanut butter cups, unwrapped

Drizzle

> 1 cup peanut butter chips

1. Heat oven to 350°F. Place sheets of foil on countertop for cooling cookies.

2. For cookies, combine chocolate chips and chocolate squares in microwave-safe measuring cup or bowl. Microwave at 50% power (MEDIUM). Stir after 2 minutes. Repeat until smooth (or melt on rangetop in small saucepan over very low heat). Cool slightly.

continued on page 36

Chocolate Peanut Butter
Cup Cookies

Chocolate Peanut Butter Cup Cookies, *continued*

3. Combine sugar and ½ cup shortening in large bowl. Beat at medium speed of electric mixer until blended and crumbly. Beat in eggs, one at a time, then salt and vanilla. Reduce speed to low. Add chocolate slowly. Mix until well blended. Stir in flour and baking soda with spoon until well blended. Shape dough into 1¼-inch balls. Roll in nuts. Place 2 inches apart on ungreased baking sheet.

4. Bake at 350°F for 8 to 10 minutes or until set. *Do not overbake*. Press peanut butter cup into center of each cookie immediately. Cool 2 minutes on baking sheet. Remove cookies to foil to cool completely.

5. For drizzle, place peanut butter chips in heavy resealable sandwich bag. Seal. Microwave at 50% power (MEDIUM). Knead bag after 1 minute. Repeat until smooth (or melt by placing bag in hot water). Cut tiny tip off corner of bag. Squeeze out and drizzle over cookies.

Makes 3 dozen cookies

Raisin Spice Drops

¾ cup (1½ sticks) margarine, softened

⅔ cup granulated sugar

⅔ cup firmly packed brown sugar

2 eggs

1 teaspoon vanilla

2½ cups QUAKER® Oats (quick or old fashioned, uncooked)

1¼ cups all-purpose flour

1 teaspoon ground cinnamon

½ teaspoon baking soda

½ teaspoon salt (optional)

¼ teaspoon ground nutmeg

⅔ cup raisins

½ cup chopped nuts

Preheat oven to 350°F. In large bowl, beat margarine and sugars until fluffy. Blend in eggs and vanilla. Add remaining ingredients; mix well. Drop dough by rounded teaspoonfuls onto ungreased cookie sheets. Bake 8 to 10 minutes or until light golden brown. Cool on wire rack. Store tightly covered.   *Makes about 4½ dozen*

Tiny Mini Kisses Peanut Blossoms

¾ cup REESE'S® Creamy Peanut Butter

½ cup shortening

⅓ cup granulated sugar

⅓ cup packed light brown sugar

1 egg

3 tablespoons milk

1 teaspoon vanilla extract

1½ cups all-purpose flour

½ teaspoon baking soda

½ teaspoon salt

Granulated sugar

HERSHEY'S® MINI KISSES™ Semi-Sweet

or Milk Chocolates

1. Heat oven to 350°F.

2. Beat peanut butter and shortening in large bowl with mixer until well mixed. Add ⅓ cup granulated sugar and brown sugar; beat well. Add egg, milk and vanilla; beat until fluffy. Stir together flour, baking soda and salt; gradually add to peanut butter mixture, beating until blended. Shape into ½-inch balls. Roll in granulated sugar; place on ungreased cookie sheet.

3. Bake 5 to 6 minutes or until set. Immediately press Mini Kiss™ into center of each cookie. Remove cookies to wire rack.   *Makes about 14 dozen cookies*

Tiny Mini Kisses Peanut Blossoms

Best-Selling Bar Cookies

No-Bake Chocolate Peanut Butter Bars

2 cups peanut butter, *divided*
¾ cup (1½ sticks) butter, softened
2 cups powdered sugar, *divided*
3 cups graham cracker crumbs
2 cups (12-ounce package) NESTLÉ® TOLL HOUSE® Semi-Sweet Chocolate Mini Morsels, *divided*

GREASE 13×9-inch baking pan.

BEAT 1¼ cups peanut butter and butter in large mixer bowl until creamy. Gradually beat in *1 cup* powdered sugar. With hands or wooden spoon, work in *remaining* powdered sugar, graham cracker crumbs and ½ *cup* morsels. Press evenly into prepared pan. Smooth top with spatula.

MELT *remaining* peanut butter and *remaining* morsels in medium, *heavy-duty* saucepan over *lowest possible heat*, stirring constantly, until smooth. Spread over graham cracker crust in pan. Refrigerate for at least 1 hour or until chocolate is firm; cut into bars. Store in refrigerator.

Makes about 5 dozen bars

No-Bake Chocolate
Peanut Butter Bars

40

Apple Golden Raisin Cheesecake Bars

1½ cups rolled oats

¾ cup all-purpose flour

½ cup firmly packed light brown sugar

¾ cup plus 2 tablespoons granulated sugar, divided

¾ Butter Flavor CRISCO® Stick or ¾ cup Butter Flavor CRISCO® all-vegetable shortening

2 (8-ounce) packages cream cheese, softened

2 large eggs

1 teaspoon vanilla

1 cup chopped Granny Smith apples

½ cup golden raisins

1 teaspoon almond extract

½ teaspoon ground cinnamon

¼ teaspoon ground nutmeg

¼ teaspoon ground allspice

1. Heat oven to 350°F.

2. Combine oats, flour, brown sugar and ¼ cup granulated sugar in large bowl; mix well. Cut in shortening with fork until crumbs form. Reserve 1 cup mixture.

3. Spray 13×9-inch baking pan with CRISCO® No-Stick Cooking Spray. Press remaining mixture onto bottom of prepared pan. Bake at 350°F for 12 to 15 minutes or until mixture is set. *Do not brown.* Place on cooling rack.

continued on page 44

Apple Golden Raisin
Cheesecake Bars

Apple Golden Raisin Cheesecake Bars, continued

4. Combine cream cheese, eggs, ½ cup granulated sugar and vanilla in large bowl. Beat at medium speed with electric mixer until well blended. Spread evenly over crust.

5. Combine apples and raisins in medium bowl. Add almond extract; stir. Add 2 tablespoons sugar, cinnamon, nutmeg and allspice; mix well. Top cream cheese mixture evenly with apple mixture; sprinkle reserved oat mixture evenly over top. Bake at 350°F for 20 to 25 minutes or until top is golden. Place on cooling rack; cool completely. Cut into bars.   *Makes 18 bars*

Kitchen Hint: Forgot to take the cream cheese out to soften? Don't worry, simply remove it from the wrapper and place it in a medium microwave-safe bowl. Microwave on MEDIUM (50% power) 15 to 20 seconds or until slightly softened.

Chippy Chewy Bars

½ cup (1 stick) butter or margarine

1½ cups graham cracker crumbs

1⅔ cups (10-ounce package) REESE'S® Peanut Butter Chips, divided

1½ cups MOUNDS® Sweetened Coconut Flakes

1 can (14 ounces) sweetened condensed milk (not evaporated milk)

1 cup HERSHEY'S Semi-Sweet Chocolate Chips or HERSHEY'S MINI CHIPS™ Semi-Sweet Chocolate Chips

1½ teaspoons shortening (do *not* use butter, margarine, spread or oil)

1. Heat oven to 350°F.

2. Place butter in 13×9×2-inch baking pan. Heat in oven until melted. Remove pan from oven. Sprinkle graham cracker crumbs evenly over butter; press down with fork. Layer 1 cup peanut butter chips over crumbs; sprinkle with coconut. Layer remaining ⅓ cup peanut butter chips over coconut; drizzle sweetened condensed milk evenly over top. Press down firmly.

3. Bake 20 minutes or until lightly browned.

4. Place chocolate chips and shortening in microwave-safe bowl. Microwave at HIGH (100%) 1 minute; stir. If necessary, microwave at HIGH an additional 15 seconds at a time, stirring after each heating, just until chips are melted when stirred. Drizzle over bars. Cool completely in pan on wire rack. Cut into bars. *Makes about 48 bars*

Note: For lighter drizzle, use ½ cup chocolate chips and ¾ teaspoon shortening. Microwave at HIGH 30 seconds to 1 minute; stir. If necessary, microwave at HIGH an additional 15 seconds at a time, stirring after each heating, just until chips are melted when stirred.

Lemon Crumb Bars

1 (18.25-ounce) package lemon or yellow cake mix
½ cup (1 stick) butter or margarine, softened
1 egg
2 cups finely crushed saltine cracker crumbs
3 egg yolks
1 (14-ounce) can EAGLE® BRAND Sweetened
    Condensed Milk (NOT evaporated milk)
½ cup lemon juice from concentrate

1. Preheat oven to 350°F. Grease 15×10×1-inch baking pan. In large mixing bowl, combine cake mix, butter and 1 egg; mix well (mixture will be crumbly). Stir in cracker crumbs. Reserve 2 cups crumb mixture. Press remaining crumb mixture firmly on bottom of prepared pan. Bake 15 minutes.

2. Meanwhile, in medium mixing bowl, combine egg yolks, Eagle Brand and lemon juice; mix well. Spread evenly over baked crust.

3. Top with reserved crumb mixture. Bake 20 minutes or until firm. Cool. Cut into bars. Store covered in refrigerator.   *Makes 3 to 4 dozen bars*

Prep Time: 30 minutes
Bake Time: 35 minutes

Lemon Crumb Bars

Chunky Pecan Pie Bars

Crust
 1½ cups all-purpose flour
  ½ cup (1 stick) butter or margarine, softened
  ¼ cup packed brown sugar

Filling
  3 large eggs
  ¾ cup corn syrup
  ¾ cup granulated sugar
  2 tablespoons butter or margarine, melted
  1 teaspoon vanilla extract
 1¾ cups (11.5-ounce package) NESTLÉ® TOLL
   HOUSE® Semi-Sweet Chocolate Chunks
 1½ cups coarsely chopped pecans

PREHEAT oven to 350°F. Grease 13×9-inch baking pan.

For Crust
BEAT flour, butter and brown sugar in small mixer bowl until crumbly. Press into prepared baking pan.

BAKE for 12 to 15 minutes or until lightly browned.

For Filling
BEAT eggs, corn syrup, granulated sugar, butter and vanilla extract in medium bowl with wire whisk. Stir in chunks and nuts. Pour evenly over baked crust.

BAKE for 25 to 30 minutes or until set. Cool completely in pan on wire rack. Cut into bars.

Makes about 3 dozen bars

Chunky Pecan Pie Bars

Cherry Cheese Bars

BASE

   1 cup walnut pieces, divided

   1¼ cups all-purpose flour

   ½ cup firmly packed brown sugar

   ½ Butter Flavor CRISCO® Stick or ½ cup Butter
      Flavor CRISCO® all-vegetable shortening
      plus additional for greasing

   ½ cup flake coconut

FILLING

   2 packages (8 ounces each) cream cheese, softened

   ⅔ cup granulated sugar

   2 eggs

   2 teaspoons vanilla

   1 can (21 ounces) cherry pie filling*

You may substitute another fruit pie filling for the cherry pie filling.

1. Heat oven to 350°F. Grease 13×9×2-inch pan with shortening. Place cooling rack on countertop.

2. Chop ½ cup nuts coarsely. Reserve for topping. Chop remaining ½ cup nuts finely.

3. For base, combine flour and brown sugar in medium bowl. Cut in shortening until fine crumbs form. Add ½ cup finely chopped nuts and coconut. Mix well. Reserve ½ cup crumbs for topping. Press remaining crumbs in bottom of pan. Bake at 350°F for 12 to 15 minutes or until edges are lightly browned. *Do not overbake*.

continued on page 52

Cherry Cheese Bars

Cherry Cheese Bars, *continued*

4. For filling, combine cream cheese, granulated sugar, eggs and vanilla in small bowl. Beat at medium speed of electric mixer until well blended. Spread over hot baked base. Return to oven. Bake 15 minutes. *Do not overbake.*

5. Spread cherry pie filling over cheese layer.

6. Combine reserved coarsely chopped nuts and reserved crumbs. Sprinkle over pie filling. Return to oven. Bake for 15 minutes. *Do not overbake.* Cool in pan on cooling rack. Refrigerate several hours. Cut into 2×1½-inch bars.

Makes 3 dozen bars

Kitchen Hint: Store brown sugar in a sealed plastic bag. It stays moist, measures easily and can be packed into a cup through the bag—no more sticky hands.

Double Chocolate Chewies

> 1 package **DUNCAN HINES®** Moist Deluxe®
> Butter Recipe Fudge Cake Mix
> 2 eggs
> ½ cup butter or margarine, melted
> 1 package (6 ounces) semisweet chocolate chips
> 1 cup chopped nuts
> Confectioners' sugar (optional)

1. Preheat oven to 350°F. Grease 13×9×2-inch pan.

2. Combine cake mix, eggs and melted butter in large bowl. Stir until well blended. (Mixture will be stiff.) Stir in chocolate chips and nuts. Press mixture evenly in prepared pan. Bake at 350°F for 25 to 30 minutes or until toothpick inserted in center comes out clean. *Do not overbake.* Cool completely. Cut into bars. Dust with confectioners' sugar, if desired. *Makes 36 bars*

Marvelous Cookie Bars

½ cup (1 stick) butter or margarine, softened

1 cup firmly packed light brown sugar

2 large eggs

1⅓ cups all-purpose flour

1 cup quick-cooking or old-fashioned oats, uncooked

⅓ cup unsweetened cocoa powder

1 teaspoon baking powder

½ teaspoon salt

¼ teaspoon baking soda

½ cup chopped walnuts, divided

1 cup "M&M's"® Semi-Sweet Chocolate Mini Baking Bits, divided

½ cup cherry preserves

¼ cup shredded coconut

Preheat oven to 350°F. Lightly grease 9×9×2-inch baking pan; set aside. In large bowl cream butter and sugar until light and fluffy; beat in eggs. In medium bowl combine flour, oats, cocoa powder, baking powder, salt and baking soda; blend into creamed mixture. Stir in ¼ cup nuts and ¾ cup "M&M's"® Semi-Sweet Chocolate Mini Baking Bits. Reserve 1 cup dough; spread remaining dough into prepared pan. Combine preserves, coconut and remaining ¼ cup nuts; spread evenly over dough to within ½ inch of edge. Drop reserved dough by rounded teaspoonfuls over preserves mixture; sprinkle with remaining ¼ cup "M&M's"® Semi-Sweet Chocolate Mini Baking Bits. Bake 25 to 30 minutes or until slightly firm near edges. Cool completely. Cut into bars. Store in tightly covered container. *Makes 16 bars*

Peanut Butter Chips and Jelly Bars

1½ cups all-purpose flour
½ cup sugar
¾ teaspoon baking powder
½ cup (1 stick) cold butter or margarine
1 egg, beaten
¾ cup grape jelly
1⅔ cups (10-ounce package) REESE'S® Peanut Butter Chips, divided

1. Heat oven to 375°F. Grease 9-inch square baking pan.

2. Stir together flour, sugar and baking powder in large bowl. With pastry blender or two knives, cut in butter until mixture resembles coarse crumbs. Add egg; blend well. Reserve 1 cup mixture; press remaining mixture onto bottom of prepared pan. Stir jelly to soften; spread evenly over crust. Sprinkle 1 cup peanut butter chips over jelly. Stir together reserved crumb mixture with remaining ⅔ cup chips; sprinkle over top.

3. Bake 25 to 30 minutes or until lightly browned. Cool completely in pan on wire rack. Cut into bars.

Makes about 16 bars

Tip: For a whimsical twist on this tried-and-true classic, use cookie cutters to cut out shapes for added fun.

Peanut Butter Chips and
Jelly Bars

White Chocolate Squares

1 (12-ounce) package white chocolate chips, divided
¼ cup (½ stick) butter or margarine
1 (14-ounce) can EAGLE® BRAND Sweetened
    Condensed Milk (NOT evaporated milk)
1 egg
1 teaspoon vanilla extract
2 cups all-purpose flour
½ teaspoon baking powder
1 cup chopped pecans, toasted
Powdered sugar

1. Preheat oven to 350°F. Grease 13×9-inch baking pan. In large saucepan over low heat, melt 1 cup chips and butter. Stir in Eagle Brand, egg and vanilla. Stir in flour and baking powder until blended. Stir in pecans and remaining chips. Spoon mixture into prepared pan.

2. Bake 20 to 25 minutes. Cool. Sprinkle with powdered sugar; cut into squares. Store covered at room temperature. *Makes 24 squares*

Prep Time: 15 minutes
Bake Time: 20 to 25 minutes

Mini Kisses Coconut Macaroon Bars

3¾ cups (10-ounce package) MOUNDS® Sweetened
    Coconut Flakes
¾ cup sugar
¼ cup all-purpose flour
¼ teaspoon salt
3 egg whites
1 whole egg, slightly beaten
1 teaspoon almond extract
1 cup HERSHEY₀S MINI KISSES™ Milk
    Chocolates

1. Heat oven to 350°F. Lightly grease 9-inch square
baking pan.

2. Stir together coconut, sugar, flour and salt in large
bowl. Add egg whites, whole egg and almond extract; stir
until well blended. Stir in Mini Kisses™. Spread mixture
into prepared pan, covering all chocolate pieces with
coconut mixture.

3. Bake 35 minutes or until lightly browned. Cool
completely in pan on wire rack. Cover with foil; allow to
stand at room temperature about 8 hours or overnight.
Cut into bars.   *Makes about 24 bars*

Prep Time: 15 minutes
Bake Time: 35 minutes
Cool Time: 9 hours

**Mini Kisses Coconut
Macaroon Bars**

Chocolatey Raspberry Crumb Bars

1 cup (2 sticks) butter or margarine, softened

2 cups all-purpose flour

½ cup packed light brown sugar

¼ teaspoon salt

2 cups (12-ounce package) NESTLÉ® TOLL HOUSE® Semi-Sweet Chocolate Morsels, *divided*

1 can (14 ounces) NESTLÉ® CARNATION® Sweetened Condensed Milk

½ cup chopped nuts (optional)

⅓ cup seedless raspberry jam

PREHEAT oven to 350°F. Grease 13×9-inch baking pan.

BEAT butter in large mixer bowl until creamy. Beat in flour, sugar and salt until crumbly. With floured fingers, press *1¾ cups* crumb mixture onto bottom of prepared baking pan; reserve *remaining* mixture.

BAKE for 10 to 12 minutes or until edges are golden brown.

MICROWAVE *1 cup* morsels and sweetened condensed milk in medium microwave-safe bowl on HIGH (100%) power for 1 minute; stir. Microwave at additional 10 to 20-second intervals, stirring until smooth. Spread over hot crust.

continued on page 62

Chocolatey Raspberry
Crumb Bars

Chocolatey Raspberry Crumb Bars, continued

STIR nuts into *reserved* flour mixture; sprinkle over chocolate layer. Drop teaspoonfuls of raspberry jam over flour mixture. Sprinkle with *remaining* morsels.

BAKE for 25 to 30 minutes or until center is set. Cool in pan on wire rack. Cut into bars.   *Makes 3 dozen bars*

S'More Cookie Bars

¾ cup (1½ sticks) IMPERIAL® Spread, melted

3 cups graham cracker crumbs

1 package (6 ounces) semi-sweet chocolate chips (1 cup)

1 cup butterscotch chips

1 cup mini marshmallows

1 can (14 ounces) sweetened condensed milk

Preheat oven to 350°F.

In 13×9-inch baking pan, combine Imperial Spread with crumbs; press to form even layer. Evenly sprinkle with chocolate chips, then butterscotch chips, then marshmallows. Pour condensed milk evenly over mixture.

Bake 25 minutes or until bubbly. On wire rack, let cool completely. To serve, cut into squares. For firmer bars, refrigerate 1 hour.   *Makes 2 dozen bars*

Razzle-Dazzle Apple
Streusel Bars

Crust and Streusel

> 2 cups QUAKER® Oats (quick or old fashioned,
>   uncooked)
>
> 2½ cups all-purpose flour
>
> 1¼ cups sugar
>
> 2 teaspoons baking powder
>
> 1 cup (2 sticks) margarine or butter, melted

Filling

> 3 cups peeled, thinly sliced apples (about 3 medium)
>
> 2 tablespoons all-purpose flour
>
> 1 (12-ounce) jar (1 cup) raspberry or apricot
>   preserves

Heat oven to 375°F. For crust and streusel, combine oats,
flour, sugar and baking powder; mix well. Add margarine,
mixing until moistened. Reserve 2 cups; set aside. Press
remaining oat mixture onto bottom of 13×9-inch baking
pan. Bake 15 minutes.

For filling, combine apples and flour. Stir in preserves.
Spread onto crust to within ½ inch of edge. Sprinkle
with reserved oat mixture, pressing lightly. Bake 30 to
35 minutes or until light golden brown. Cool completely;
cut into bars. Store tightly covered.

Makes 2 dozen bars

Marbled Cheesecake Bars

2 cups finely crushed crème-filled chocolate
sandwich cookie crumbs (about 24 cookies)

3 tablespoons butter or margarine, melted

3 (8-ounce) packages cream cheese, softened

1 (14-ounce) can EAGLE® BRAND Sweetened
Condensed Milk (NOT evaporated milk)

3 eggs

2 teaspoons vanilla extract

2 (1-ounce) squares unsweetened chocolate, melted

1. Preheat oven to 300°F. Line 13×9-inch baking pan
with heavy foil; set aside. In medium bowl, combine
crumbs and butter; press firmly on bottom of prepared pan.

2. In large bowl, beat cream cheese until fluffy. Gradually
beat in Eagle Brand until smooth. Add eggs and vanilla;
mix well. Pour half the batter evenly over prepared crust.

3. Stir melted chocolate into remaining batter; spoon
over vanilla batter. With table knife or metal spatula,
gently swirl through batter to marble.

4. Bake 45 to 50 minutes or until set. Cool. Chill. Cut
into bars. Store covered in refrigerator.

Makes 2 to 3 dozen bars

Tip: For even marbling, do not oversoften or overbeat the
cream cheese.

Prep Time: 20 minutes
Bake Time: 45 to 50 minutes

Marbled Cheesecake Bars

Chocolate Chip Candy Cookie Bars

1⅔ cups all-purpose flour

2 tablespoons plus 1½ cups sugar, divided

¾ teaspoon baking powder

1 cup (2 sticks) cold butter or margarine, divided

1 egg, slightly beaten

½ cup plus 2 tablespoons (5-ounce can) evaporated milk, divided

2 cups (12-ounce package) HERSHEY'S Semi-Sweet Chocolate Chips, divided

½ cup light corn syrup

1½ cups sliced almonds

1. Heat oven to 375°F. Combine flour, 2 tablespoons sugar and baking powder in medium bowl; using pastry blender, cut in ½ cup butter until mixture forms coarse crumbs. Stir in egg and 2 tablespoons evaporated milk; stir until mixture holds together in ball shape. Press onto bottom and ¼ inch up sides of 15½×10½×1-inch jelly-roll pan.

2. Bake 8 to 10 minutes or until lightly browned; remove from oven, leaving oven on. Sprinkle 1½ cups chocolate chips evenly over crust; do not disturb chips.

3. Place remaining 1½ cups sugar, remaining ½ cup butter, remaining ½ cup evaporated milk and corn syrup in 3-quart saucepan. Cook over medium heat, stirring constantly, until mixture boils; stir in almonds. Continue

continued on page 68

Chocolate Chip Candy
Cookie Bars

Chocolate Chip Candy Cookie Bars, *continued*

cooking and stirring to 240°F on candy thermometer (soft-ball stage) or until small amount of mixture, when dropped into very cold water, forms a soft ball which flattens when removed from water. (Bulb of candy thermometer should not rest on bottom of saucepan.) Remove from heat. Immediately spoon almond mixture evenly over chips and crust; do not spread.

4. Bake 10 to 15 minutes or just until almond mixture is golden brown. Remove from oven; cool 5 minutes. Sprinkle remaining ½ cup chips over top; cool completely. Cut into bars.   *Makes about 48 bars*

Buttery Black Raspberry Bars

----

    1 cup butter or margarine
    1 cup sugar
    2 egg yolks
    2 cups all-purpose flour
    1 cup chopped walnuts
    ½ cup SMUCKER'S® Seedless Black Raspberry Jam

Beat butter until soft and creamy. Gradually add sugar, beating until mixture is light and fluffy. Add egg yolks; blend well. Gradually add flour; mix thoroughly. Fold in walnuts.

Spoon half of batter into greased 8-inch square pan; spread evenly. Top with jam; cover with remaining batter.

Bake at 325°F for 1 hour or until lightly browned. Cool and cut into 2×1-inch bars.   *Makes 32 bars*

Fabulous Fruit Bars

1½ **cups all-purpose flour, divided**
1½ **cups sugar, divided**
  ½ **cup MOTT'S® Apple Sauce, divided**
  ½ **teaspoon baking powder**
  2 **tablespoons margarine**
  ½ **cup chopped peeled apple**
  ½ **cup chopped dried apricots**
  ½ **cup chopped cranberries**
  1 **whole egg**
  1 **egg white**
  1 **teaspoon lemon juice**
  ½ **teaspoon vanilla extract**
  1 **teaspoon ground cinnamon**

1. Preheat oven to 350°F. Spray 13×9-inch baking pan with nonstick cooking spray.

2. In medium bowl, combine 1¼ cups flour, ½ cup sugar, ⅓ cup apple sauce and baking powder. Cut in margarine with fork until mixture resembles coarse crumbs.

3. In large bowl, combine apple, apricots, cranberries, remaining apple sauce, whole egg, egg white, lemon juice and vanilla.

4. In small bowl, combine remaining 1 cup sugar, ¼ cup flour and cinnamon. Add to fruit mixture, stirring just until mixed.

5. Press half of crumb mixture evenly into bottom of prepared pan. Top with fruit mixture. Sprinkle with remaining crumb mixture.

6. Bake 40 minutes or until lightly browned. Broil, 4 inches from heat, 1 to 2 minutes or until golden brown. Cool on wire rack 15 minutes; cut into 16 bars.

Makes 16 servings

Rocky Road Bars

2 cups (12-ounce package) NESTLÉ® TOLL
HOUSE® Semi-Sweet Chocolate Morsels,
divided

1½ cups all-purpose flour

1½ teaspoons baking powder

1 cup granulated sugar

6 tablespoons (¾ stick) butter or margarine,
softened

1½ teaspoons vanilla extract

2 large eggs

2 cups miniature marshmallows

1½ cups coarsely chopped walnuts

PREHEAT oven to 375°F. Grease 13×9-inch baking pan.

MICROWAVE *1 cup* morsels in medium, microwave-safe bowl on HIGH (100%) power for 1 minute; stir. Microwave at additional 10- to 20-second intervals; stir until smooth. Cool to room temperature. Combine flour and baking powder in small bowl.

BEAT sugar, butter and vanilla in large mixer bowl until crumbly. Beat in eggs. Add melted chocolate; beat until smooth. Gradually beat in flour mixture. Spread batter into prepared baking pan.

BAKE for 16 to 20 minutes or until wooden pick inserted in center comes out slightly sticky.

REMOVE from oven; sprinkle immediately with marshmallows, nuts and *remaining* morsels. Return to oven for 2 minutes or just until marshmallows begin to melt. Cool in pan on wire rack 20 to 30 minutes. Cut into bars with wet knife. Serve warm.   *Makes 2½ dozen bars*

Rocky Road Bars

Chocolate Nut Bars

1¾ cups graham cracker crumbs

½ cup (1 stick) butter or margarine, melted

1 (14-ounce) can EAGLE® BRAND Sweetened Condensed Milk (NOT evaporated milk)

2 cups (12 ounces) semi-sweet chocolate chips, divided

1 teaspoon vanilla extract

1 cup chopped nuts

1. Preheat oven to 375°F. In medium mixing bowl, combine crumbs and butter; press firmly on bottom of ungreased 13×9-inch baking pan. Bake 8 minutes. Reduce oven temperature to 350°F.

2. In small saucepan, melt Eagle Brand with 1 cup chips and vanilla. Spread chocolate mixture over prepared crust. Top with remaining 1 cup chips and nuts; press down firmly.

3. Bake 25 to 30 minutes. Cool. Chill, if desired. Cut into bars. Store loosely covered at room temperature.

Makes 24 to 36 bars

Prep Time: 10 minutes
Bake Time: 33 to 38 minutes

Chocolate Nut Bars

Blue-Ribbon Brownies

Hershey's Best Brownies

1 cup (2 sticks) butter or margarine

2 cups sugar

2 teaspoons vanilla extract

4 eggs

¾ cup HERSHEY'S Cocoa or HERSHEY'S Dutch
   Processed Cocoa

1 cup all-purpose flour

½ teaspoon baking powder

¼ teaspoon salt

1 cup chopped nuts (optional)

1. Heat oven to 350°F. Grease 13×9×2-inch baking pan.

2. Place butter in large microwave-safe bowl. Microwave at HIGH (100%) 2 to 2½ minutes or until melted. Stir in sugar and vanilla. Add eggs, one at a time, beating well with spoon after each addition. Add cocoa; beat until well blended. Add flour, baking powder and salt; beat well. Stir in nuts, if desired. Pour batter into prepared pan.

3. Bake 30 to 35 minutes or until brownies begin to pull away from sides of pan. Cool completely in pan on wire rack. Cut into bars.   *Makes about 36 brownies*

Hershey's Best Brownies

Oatmeal Brownie Gems

2¾ cups quick-cooking or old-fashioned oats,
   uncooked
1 cup all-purpose flour
1 cup firmly packed light brown sugar
1 cup coarsely chopped walnuts
1 teaspoon baking soda
1 cup butter or margarine, melted
1¾ cups "M&M's"® Semi-Sweet Chocolate
   Mini Baking Bits
1 (19- to 21-ounce) package fudge brownie mix,
   prepared according to package directions
   for fudge-like brownies

Preheat oven to 350°F. In large bowl combine oats, flour,
sugar, nuts and baking soda; add butter until mixture
forms coarse crumbs. Stir in "M&M's"® Semi-Sweet
Chocolate Mini Baking Bits until evenly distributed.
Reserve 3 cups mixture. Pat remaining mixture onto
bottom of 15×10×1-inch pan to form crust. Pour
prepared brownie mix over crust, carefully spreading into
thin layer. Sprinkle reserved crumb mixture over top of
brownie mixture; pat down lightly. Bake 25 to 30 minutes
or until toothpick inserted in center comes out with moist
crumbs. Cool completely. Cut into bars. Store in tightly
covered container.   *Makes 48 bars*

Oatmeal Brownie Gems

Recipe for Oatmeal Brow

From — Josephine

Ser

Ingredients:

2 3/4 cups quick-cooking or old
fashioned oats, uncooked
1 cup all-purpose flour
1 cup firmly packed brown sugar
1 tsp. baking soda
1 cup c   uts

Blue-Ribbon
Brownies

Toffee Brownie Bars

Crust
   ¾ cup butter or margarine, softened
   ¾ cup firmly packed brown sugar
   1 egg yolk
   ¾ teaspoon vanilla extract
   1½ cups all-purpose flour

Filling
   1 (21-ounce) package DUNCAN HINES®
      Family-Style Chewy Fudge Brownie Mix
   1 egg
   ⅓ cup water
   ⅓ cup vegetable oil

Topping
   1 package (12 ounces) milk chocolate chips, melted
   ¾ cup finely chopped pecans

1. Preheat oven to 350°F. Grease 15½×10½×1-inch pan.

2. For crust, combine butter, brown sugar, egg yolk and vanilla extract in large bowl. Stir in flour. Spread in prepared pan. Bake at 350°F 15 minutes or until golden.

3. For filling, prepare brownie mix following package directions. Spread over hot crust. Bake at 350°F for 15 minutes or until surface appears set. Cool 30 minutes.

4. For topping, spread melted chocolate on top of brownie layer; sprinkle with pecans. Cool completely.

Makes 48 bars

Miniature Brownie Cups

6 tablespoons butter or margarine, melted

¾ cup sugar

½ teaspoon vanilla extract

2 eggs

½ cup all-purpose flour

¼ cup HERSHEY'S Cocoa or HERSHEY'S
      Dutch Processed Cocoa

¼ teaspoon baking powder

   Dash salt

¼ cup finely chopped nuts

1. Heat oven to 350°F. Line small muffin cups (1¾ inches in diameter) with paper bake cups. Stir together butter, sugar and vanilla in medium bowl. Add eggs; beat well with spoon.

2. Stir together flour, cocoa, baking powder and salt; gradually add to butter mixture, beating with spoon until well blended. Fill muffin cups ½ full with batter; sprinkle nuts over top.

3. Bake 12 to 15 minutes or until wooden pick inserted in center comes out almost clean. Cool slightly; remove brownies from pan to wire rack. Cool completely.

Makes about 24 brownies

Prep Time: 20 minutes
Bake Time: 12 minutes
Cool Time: 25 minutes

Scrumptious Minted Brownies

1 (21-ounce) package DUNCAN HINES®
Family-Style Chewy Fudge Brownie Mix

1 egg

⅓ cup water

⅓ cup vegetable oil

48 chocolate crème de menthe candy wafers, divided

1. Preheat oven to 350°F. Grease bottom only of 13×9-inch pan.

2. Combine brownie mix, egg, water and oil in large bowl. Stir with spoon until well blended, about 50 strokes. Spread in prepared pan. Bake at 350°F for 25 minutes or until set. Place 30 candy wafers evenly over hot brownies. Let stand for 1 minute to melt. Spread candy wafers to frost brownies. Score frosting into 36 bars by running tip of knife through melted candy. (Do not cut through brownies.) Cut remaining 18 candy wafers in half lengthwise; place halves on each scored bar. Cool completely. Cut into bars.   *Makes 36 brownies*

Scrumptious Minted
Brownies

Decadent Blonde Brownies

1½ cups all-purpose flour

1 teaspoon baking powder

½ teaspoon salt

¾ cup granulated sugar

¾ cup packed light brown sugar

½ cup (1 stick) butter, softened

2 large eggs

2 teaspoons vanilla

1 package (10 ounces) semisweet chocolate chunks*

1 jar (3½ ounces) macadamia nuts, coarsely
   chopped, to measure ¾ cup

*If chocolate chunks are not available, cut 1 (10-ounce) thick chocolate candy
bar into ½-inch pieces to equal 1½ cups.*

Preheat oven to 350°F. Grease 13×9-inch baking pan.
Combine flour, baking powder and salt in small bowl;
set aside.

Beat granulated sugar, brown sugar and butter in large
bowl with electric mixer at medium speed until light and
fluffy. Beat in eggs and vanilla. Add flour mixture. Beat at
low speed until well blended. Stir in chocolate chunks and
macadamia nuts. Spread batter evenly into prepared pan.
Bake 25 to 30 minutes or until golden brown. Remove pan
to wire rack; cool completely. Cut into 3¼×1½-inch bars.

Makes 2 dozen brownies

Decadent Blonde Brownies

Creamy Filled Brownies

½ cup (1 stick) butter or margarine
⅓ cup HERSHEY'S Cocoa
2 eggs
1 cup sugar
½ cup all-purpose flour
¼ teaspoon baking powder
¼ teaspoon salt
1 teaspoon vanilla extract
1 cup finely chopped nuts
   Creamy Filling (page 86)
   MiniChip Glaze (page 86)
½ cup sliced almonds or chopped nuts (optional)

1. Heat oven to 350°F. Line 15½×10½×1-inch jelly-roll pan with foil; grease foil.

2. Melt butter in small saucepan; remove from heat. Stir in cocoa until smooth. Beat eggs in medium bowl; gradually add sugar, beating until fluffy. Stir together flour, baking powder and salt; add to egg mixture. Add cocoa mixture and vanilla; beat well. Stir in nuts. Spread batter into prepared pan.

3. Bake 12 to 14 minutes or until top springs back when touched lightly in center. Cool completely in pan on wire rack; remove from pan to cutting board. Remove foil; cut brownie in half crosswise. Spread one half with Creamy

continued on page 86

Creamy Filled Brownie

Creamy Filled Brownies, *continued*

Filling; top with second half. Spread MiniChip Glaze over top; sprinkle with almonds, if desired. After glaze has set cut into bars. *Makes about 24 brownies*

Creamy Filling: Beat 1 package (3 ounces) softened cream cheese, 2 tablespoons softened butter or margarine and 1 teaspoon vanilla extract in small bowl. Gradually add 1½ cups powdered sugar, beating until of spreading consistency.

MiniChip Glaze: Heat ¼ cup sugar and 2 tablespoons water to boiling in small saucepan. Remove from heat. Immediately add ½ cup HERSHEY'S MINICHIPS™ Semi-Sweet Chocolate, stirring until melted.

Filling Variations: Coffee: Add 1 teaspoon powdered instant coffee. Orange: Add ½ teaspoon freshly grated orange peel and 1 or 2 drops orange food color. Almond: Add ¼ teaspoon almond extract.

Mississippi Mud Brownies

1 (21-ounce) package DUNCAN HINES®
    Family-Style Chewy Fudge Brownie Mix
2 eggs
⅓ cup water
⅓ cup vegetable oil plus additional for greasing
1 jar (7 ounces) marshmallow creme
1 container DUNCAN HINES® Milk Chocolate
    Frosting, melted

1. Preheat oven to 350°F. Grease bottom only of
13×9-inch pan.

2. Combine brownie mix, eggs, water and oil in large
bowl. Stir with spoon until well blended, about 50 strokes.
Spread in pan. Bake at 350°F for 25 to 28 minutes or
until set.

3. Spread marshmallow creme gently over hot brownies.
Pour 1¼ cups melted milk chocolate frosting over
marshmallow creme. Swirl with knife to marble. Cool
completely. Cut into bars.   *Makes 20 to 24 brownies*

Note: Store leftover melted frosting in original container.
Refrigerate.

Coconutty "M&M's"® Brownies

6 squares (1 ounce each) semi-sweet chocolate

¾ cup granulated sugar

½ cup (1 stick) butter

2 large eggs

1 tablespoon vegetable oil

1 teaspoon vanilla extract

1¼ cups all-purpose flour

3 tablespoons unsweetened cocoa powder

1 teaspoon baking powder

½ teaspoon salt

1½ cups "M&M's"® Chocolate Mini Baking Bits, divided

Coconut Topping (page 90)

Preheat oven to 350°F. Lightly grease 8×8×2-inch baking pan; set aside. In small saucepan combine chocolate, sugar and butter over low heat; stir constantly until chocolate is melted. Remove from heat; let cool slightly. In large bowl beat eggs, oil and vanilla; stir in chocolate mixture until well blended. In medium bowl combine flour, cocoa powder, baking powder and salt; add to chocolate mixture. Stir in 1 cup "M&M's"® Chocolate Mini Baking Bits. Spread batter evenly in prepared pan. Bake 35 to 40 minutes or until toothpick inserted in center comes

continued on page 90

Coconutty "M&M's"®
Brownies

88

Coconutty "M&M's"® Brownies, *continued*

out clean. Cool completely on wire rack. Prepare Coconut
Topping. Spread over brownies; sprinkle with remaining
½ cup "M&M's"® Chocolate Mini Baking Bits. Cut into
bars. Store in tightly covered container.

Makes 16 brownies

Coconut Topping

½ cup (1 stick) butter
⅓ cup firmly packed light brown sugar
⅓ cup light corn syrup
1 cup sweetened shredded coconut, toasted*
¾ cup chopped pecans
1 teaspoon vanilla extract

**To toast coconut, spread evenly on cookie sheet. Toast in preheated 350°F oven
7 to 8 minutes or until golden brown, stirring occasionally.*

In large saucepan melt butter over medium heat; add
brown sugar and corn syrup, stirring constantly until
thick and bubbly. Remove from heat and stir in
remaining ingredients.

Double Mint Brownies

1 (21-ounce) package DUNCAN HINES®
    Family-Style Chewy Recipe Fudge Brownie Mix

1 egg

⅓ cup water

⅓ cup vegetable oil plus additional for greasing

½ teaspoon peppermint extract

24 chocolate-covered peppermint patties
    (1½ inches each)

1 cup confectioners' sugar, divided

4 teaspoons milk, divided

    Red food coloring

    Green food coloring

1. Preheat oven to 350°F. Grease bottom only of
13×9×2-inch pan. Combine brownie mix, egg, water,
oil and peppermint extract in large bowl. Stir with spoon
until well blended, about 50 strokes. Spread in prepared
pan. Bake brownies following package directions. Place
peppermint patties on warm brownies. Cool completely.

2. Combine ½ cup confectioners' sugar, 2 teaspoons
milk and 1 drop red food coloring in small bowl. Stir
until smooth. Place in small resealable plastic bag; set
aside. Repeat with remaining ½ cup confectioners' sugar,
remaining 2 teaspoons milk and 1 drop green food
coloring. Cut pinpoint hole in bottom corner of each
bag. Drizzle pink and green glazes over brownies. Allow
glazes to set before cutting into bars.

Makes 24 brownies

Tip: To prevent overdone edges and underdone center,
wrap foil strips around outside edges of pan (do not cover
bottom or top). Bake as directed above.

Cheesecake-Topped Brownies

1 (21.5- or 23.6-ounce) package fudge brownie mix
1 (8-ounce) package cream cheese, softened
2 tablespoons butter or margarine, softened
1 tablespoon cornstarch
1 (14-ounce) can EAGLE® BRAND Sweetened Condensed Milk (NOT evaporated milk)
1 egg
2 teaspoons vanilla extract
Ready-to-spread chocolate frosting, if desired
Orange peel, if desired

1. Preheat oven to 350°F. Prepare brownie mix as package directs. Spread into well-greased 13×9-inch baking pan.

2. In large mixing bowl, beat cream cheese, butter and cornstarch until fluffy.

3. Gradually beat in Eagle Brand. Add egg and vanilla; beat until smooth. Pour cheesecake mixture evenly over brownie batter.

4. Bake 40 to 45 minutes or until top is lightly browned. Cool. Spread with frosting or sprinkle with orange peel, if desired. Cut into bars. Store covered in refrigerator.

Makes 3 to 3½ dozen brownies

Prep Time: 20 minutes
Bake Time: 40 to 45 minutes

Cheesecake-Topped
Brownies

Easy Double Chocolate Chip Brownies

2 cups (12-ounce package) NESTLÉ® TOLL
   HOUSE® Semi-Sweet Chocolate Morsels,
   divided

½ cup (1 stick) butter or margarine, cut into pieces

3 large eggs

1¼ cups all-purpose flour

1 cup granulated sugar

1 teaspoon vanilla extract

¼ teaspoon baking soda

½ cup chopped nuts

PREHEAT oven to 350°F. Grease 13×9-inch baking pan.

MELT *1 cup* morsels and butter in large, *heavy-duty* saucepan over low heat; stir until smooth. Remove from heat. Stir in eggs. Stir in flour, sugar, vanilla extract and baking soda. Stir in *remaining* morsels and nuts. Spread into prepared baking pan.

BAKE for 18 to 22 minutes or until wooden pick inserted in center comes out slightly sticky. Cool completely in pan on wire rack. *Makes 2 dozen brownies*

Easy Double Chocolate
Chip Brownies

Hershey's White Chip Brownies

4 eggs

1¼ cups sugar

½ cup (1 stick) butter or margarine, melted

2 teaspoons vanilla extract

1⅓ cups all-purpose flour

⅔ cup HERSHEY'S Cocoa

1 teaspoon baking powder

½ teaspoon salt

1⅔ cups (10-ounce package) HERSHEY'S Premier White Chips

1. Heat oven to 350°F. Grease 13×9×2-inch baking pan.

2. Beat eggs in large bowl until foamy; gradually beat in sugar. Add butter and vanilla; beat until blended. Stir together flour, cocoa, baking powder and salt; add to egg mixture, beating until blended. Stir in white chips. Spread batter into prepared pan.

3. Bake 25 to 30 minutes or until brownies begin to pull away from sides of pan. Cool completely in pan on wire rack. Cut into squares.   *Makes about 36 brownies*

Prep Time: 15 minutes
Bake Time: 25 minutes
Cool Time: 2 hours

Hershey's White Chip
Brownies

Classic Cupcakes

Touchdown Brownie Cups

1 cup (2 sticks) butter or margarine
½ cup HERSHEY'S Cocoa or HERSHEY'S
    Dutch Processed Cocoa
1 cup packed light brown sugar
½ cup granulated sugar
3 eggs
1 teaspoon vanilla extract
1 cup all-purpose flour
1⅓ cup chopped pecans, divided

1. Heat oven to 350°F. Line 2½-inch muffin cups with paper or foil bake cups.

2. Place butter in large microwave-safe bowl; cover. Microwave at HIGH (100%) 1½ minutes or until melted. Add cocoa; stir until smooth. Add sugars; stir until well blended. Add eggs and vanilla; beat well. Add flour and 1 cup pecans; stir until well blended. Fill prepared muffin cups about ¾ full with batter; sprinkle about 1 teaspoon remaining pecans over top of each.

3. Bake 20 to 25 minutes or until tops are beginning to dry and crack. Cool completely in cups on wire rack.

Makes about 17 cupcakes

Touchdown Brownie Cups

Pretty in Pink Peppermint Cupcakes

1 package (18.25 ounces) white cake mix
1⅓ cups water
3 large egg whites
2 tablespoons vegetable oil or melted butter
½ teaspoon peppermint extract
3 to 4 drops red liquid food coloring *or* ¼ teaspoon gel food coloring
1 container (16 ounces) prepared vanilla frosting
½ cup crushed peppermint candies (about 16 candies)

1. Preheat oven to 350°F. Line 30 regular-size (2½-inch) muffin pan cups with pink or white paper muffin cup liners.

2. Beat cake mix, water, egg whites, oil, peppermint extract and food coloring with electric mixer at low speed 30 seconds. Beat at medium speed 2 minutes.

3. Spoon batter into prepared cups filling ¾ full. Bake 20 to 22 minutes or until toothpick inserted into centers comes out clean. Cool in pans on wire racks 10 minutes. Remove cupcakes to racks; cool completely.

4. Spread cooled cupcakes with frosting; top with crushed candies. Store at room temperature up to 24 hours or cover and refrigerate up to 3 days before serving.

Makes about 30 cupcakes

Pretty in Pink
Peppermint Cupcakes

Captivating Caterpillar
Cupcakes

1 package DUNCAN HINES® Moist Deluxe®
   White Cake Mix

3 egg whites

1⅓ cups water

2 tablespoons vegetable oil

½ cup star decors, divided

1 container DUNCAN HINES® Vanilla Frosting
   Green food coloring

6 chocolate sandwich cookies, finely crushed
   (see Tip on page 104)

½ cup candy-coated chocolate pieces

⅓ cup assorted jelly beans
   Assorted nonpareil decors

1. Preheat oven to 350°F. Place 24 (2½-inch) paper liners in muffin cups.

2. Combine cake mix, egg whites, water and oil in large bowl. Beat at low speed with electric mixer until moistened. Beat at medium speed 2 minutes. Fold in ⅓ cup star decors. Fill paper liners about half full. Bake at 350°F for 18 to 23 minutes or until toothpick inserted in center comes out clean. Cool in pans 5 minutes. Remove to cooling racks. Cool completely.

3. Tint vanilla frosting with green food coloring. Frost one cupcake. Sprinkle ½ teaspoon chocolate cookie

continued on page 104

Captivating Caterpillar
Cupcakes

Captivating Caterpillar Cupcakes, *continued*

crumbs on frosting. Arrange 4 candy-coated chocolate pieces to form caterpillar body. Place jelly bean at one end to form head. Attach remaining star and nonpareil decors with dots of frosting to form eyes. Repeat with remaining cupcakes. *Makes 24 cupcakes*

Tip: To finely crush chocolate sandwich cookies, place cookies in resealable plastic bag. Remove excess air from bag; seal. Press rolling pin on top of cookies to break into pieces. Continue pressing until evenly crushed.

Brownie Peanut Butter Cupcakes

18 REYNOLDS® Foil Baking Cups
⅓ cup creamy peanut butter
¼ cup light cream cheese
2 tablespoons sugar
1 egg
1 package (about 19 ounces) fudge brownie mix
½ cup candy coated peanut butter candies

PREHEAT oven to 350°F. Place Reynolds Foil Baking Cups in muffin pans or on cookie sheet; set aside. Beat peanut butter, cream cheese, sugar and egg in bowl with electric mixer; set aside.

PREPARE brownie mix following package directions; set aside. Place 1 heaping teaspoon of peanut butter mixture in center of each baking cup. With spoon or small ice cream scoop, fill baking cups half full with brownie batter. Sprinkle each brownie cupcake with peanut butter candies.

BAKE 25 minutes; do not overbake. Cool.
Makes 18 brownie cupcakes

Golden Apple Cupcakes

1 package (18 to 20 ounces) yellow cake mix
1 cup MOTT'S® Chunky Apple Sauce
⅓ cup vegetable oil
3 eggs
¼ cup firmly packed light brown sugar
¼ cup chopped walnuts
½ teaspoon ground cinnamon
Vanilla Frosting (recipe follows)

Heat oven to 350°F. In bowl, combine cake mix, apple sauce, oil and eggs; blend according to package directions. Spoon batter into 24 paper-lined muffin pan cups. Mix brown sugar, walnuts and cinnamon; sprinkle over prepared batter in muffin cups. Bake 20 to 25 minutes or until toothpick inserted in center comes out clean. Cool in pan 10 minutes. Remove from pan; cool completely on wire rack. Frost cupcakes with Vanilla Frosting.

Makes 24 cupcakes

Vanilla Frosting: In large bowl, beat 1 package (8 ounces) softened cream cheese until light and creamy; blend in ¼ teaspoon vanilla extract. Beat ½ cup heavy cream until stiff; fold into cream cheese mixture.

Mini Turtle Cupcakes

1 package (21.5 ounces) brownie mix plus
     ingredients to prepare mix
½ cup chopped pecans
1 cup prepared or homemade dark chocolate frosting
½ cup chopped pecans, toasted
12 caramels, unwrapped
1 to 2 tablespoons whipping cream

1. Heat oven to 350°F. Line 54 mini (1½-inch) muffin cups with paper muffin cup liners.

2. Prepare brownie batter as directed on package. Stir in chopped pecans.

3. Spoon batter into prepared muffin cups filling ⅔ full. Bake 18 minutes or until toothpick inserted into centers comes out clean. Cool in pans on wire racks 5 minutes. Remove cupcakes to racks; cool completely. (At this point, cupcakes may be frozen up to 3 months. Thaw at room temperature before frosting.)

4. Spread frosting over cooled cupcakes; top with pecans.

5. Combine caramels and 1 tablespoon cream in small saucepan. Cook over low heat until caramels are melted and mixture is smooth, stirring constantly. Add additional 1 tablespoon cream if needed. Drizzle caramel decoratively over cupcakes. Store at room temperature up to 24 hours or cover and refrigerate for up to 3 days before serving.

Makes 54 mini cupcakes

Mini Turtle Cupcakes

Blueberry Crisp Cupcakes

Cupcakes
- 2 cups all-purpose flour
- 2 teaspoons baking powder
- ¼ teaspoon salt
- 1¾ cups granulated sugar
- ½ cup (1 stick) butter, softened
- ¾ cup milk
- 1½ teaspoons vanilla
- 3 large egg whites
- 3 cups fresh or frozen (unthawed) blueberries

Streusel
- ⅓ cup all-purpose flour
- ¼ cup uncooked old-fashioned or quick oats
- ¼ cup packed light brown sugar
- ½ teaspoon ground cinnamon
- ¼ cup butter, softened
- ½ cup chopped walnuts or pecans

1. Preheat oven to 350°F. Line 30 regular-size (2½-inch) muffin cups with paper muffin cup liners.

2. For cupcakes, combine 2 cups flour, baking powder and salt in medium bowl; mix well and set aside. Beat granulated sugar and ½ cup butter with electric mixer at medium speed 1 minute. Add milk and vanilla. Beat at low speed 30 seconds. Gradually beat in flour mixture; beat at medium speed 2 minutes. Add egg whites; beat

continued on page 110

Blueberry Crisp Cupcakes

Blueberry Crisp Cupcakes, *continued*

1 minute. Spoon batter into prepared muffin cups filling ½ full. Spoon blueberries over batter. Bake 10 minutes.

3. Meanwhile for streusel, combine ⅓ cup flour, oats, brown sugar and cinnamon in small bowl; mix well. Cut in ¼ cup butter with pastry blender or two knives until mixture is well combined. Stir in chopped nuts.

4. Sprinkle streusel over partially baked cupcakes. Return to oven; bake 18 to 20 minutes or until golden brown and toothpick inserted into centers comes out clean. Cool in pans on wire racks 10 minutes. Remove cupcakes to racks; cool completely. (Cupcakes may be frozen up to 3 months.) *Makes 30 cupcakes*

Ultimate Rocky Road Cups

¾ cup (1½ sticks) butter or margarine

4 squares (1 ounce each) unsweetened baking chocolate

1½ cups granulated sugar

3 large eggs

1 cup all-purpose flour

1¾ cups "M&M's"® Chocolate Mini Baking Bits

¾ cup coarsely chopped peanuts

1 cup mini marshmallows

Preheat oven to 350°F. Generously grease 24 (2½-inch) muffin cups or line with foil liners. Place butter and chocolate in large microwave-safe bowl. Microwave on HIGH 1 minute; stir. Microwave on HIGH an additional 30 seconds; stir until chocolate is completely melted. Add sugar and eggs, one at a time, beating well after each addition; blend in flour. In separate bowl combine "M&M's"® Chocolate Mini Baking Bits and nuts; stir 1 cup baking bits mixture into brownie batter. Divide batter evenly among prepared muffin cups. Bake 20 minutes. Combine remaining baking bits mixture with marshmallows; divide evenly among muffin cups, topping hot brownies. Return to oven; bake 5 minutes longer. Cool completely before removing from muffin cups. Store in tightly covered container. *Makes 24 cups*

Mini Ultimate Rocky Road Cups: Prepare recipe as directed, dividing batter among 60 generously greased 2-inch mini muffin cups. Bake 15 minutes. Sprinkle with topping mixture; bake 5 minutes longer. Cool completely before removing from cups. Store in tightly covered container. Makes about 60 mini cups.

Peanut Butter Surprise

2 cups all-purpose flour

2 teaspoons baking powder

¼ teaspoon salt

1¾ cups sugar

½ cup (1 stick) butter, softened

¾ cup reduced-fat (2%) or whole milk

1 teaspoon vanilla

3 large egg whites

2 (3-ounce) bittersweet chocolate candy bars, melted and cooled

30 mini peanut butter cups

1 container prepared chocolate frosting

3 ounces white chocolate candy bar, broken into chunks

1. Preheat oven to 350°F. Line 30 regular-size (2½-inch) muffin cups with paper muffin cup liners.

2. For cupcakes, combine flour, baking powder and salt in medium bowl; mix well and set aside. Beat sugar and butter with electric mixer at medium speed 1 minute. Add milk and vanilla. Beat with electric mixer at low speed 30 seconds. Gradually beat in flour mixture; beat at medium speed 2 minutes. Add egg whites; beat 1 minute. Stir in melted chocolate.

3. Spoon 1 heaping tablespoon batter into each prepared muffin cup; use back of spoon to slightly spread batter over bottom. Place one mini peanut butter cup in center of

continued on page 114

Peanut Butter Surprise

Peanut Butter Surprise, *continued*

each cupcake. Spoon 1 heaping tablespoon batter over peanut butter cup; use back of spoon to smooth out batter. (Do not fill cups more than ¾ full.)

4. Bake 24 to 26 minutes or until puffed and golden brown. Cool in pans on wire racks 10 minutes. (Center of cupcakes will sink slightly upon cooling.) Remove cupcakes to racks; cool completely. (At this point, cupcakes may be frozen up to 3 months.) Spread frosting over cooled cupcakes.

5. For white drizzle, place white chocolate in small resealable plastic food storage bag. Microwave at HIGH 30 to 40 seconds. Turn bag over; microwave additional 30 seconds or until chocolate is melted. Cut off tiny corner of bag; pipe chocolate decoratively over frosted cupcakes. Store at room temperature up to 24 hours or cover and refrigerate up to 3 days before serving.

Makes 30 cupcakes

Lemon Poppy Seed Cupcakes

Cupcakes
>   1 package DUNCAN HINES® Moist Deluxe®
>   Lemon Supreme Cake Mix
>   3 eggs
>   1⅓ cups water
>   ⅓ cup vegetable oil
>   3 tablespoons poppy seed

Lemon Frosting
>   1 container (16 ounces) DUNCAN HINES®
>   Vanilla Frosting
>   1 teaspoon grated lemon peel
>   ¼ teaspoon lemon extract
>   3 to 4 drops yellow food coloring
>   Yellow and orange gumdrops for garnish

1. Preheat oven to 350°F. Place 30 (2½-inch) paper liners in muffin cups.

2. For cupcakes, combine cake mix, eggs, water, oil and poppy seed in large bowl. Beat at medium speed of electric mixer 2 minutes. Fill paper liners about half full. Bake 18 to 21 minutes or until toothpick inserted in center comes out clean. Cool in pans 5 minutes. Remove to cooling racks. Cool completely.

3. For lemon frosting, combine Vanilla frosting, lemon peel and lemon extract in small bowl. Tint with yellow food coloring to desired color. Frost cupcakes with lemon frosting. Decorate with gumdrops.   *Makes 30 cupcakes*

Red's Rockin'
Rainbow Cupcakes

2¼ cups all-purpose flour

1 tablespoon baking powder

½ teaspoon salt

1⅔ cups granulated sugar

½ cup (1 stick) butter, softened

1 cup milk

2 teaspoons vanilla extract

3 large egg whites

Blue and assorted food colorings

1 container (16 ounces) white frosting

1½ cups "M&M's"® Chocolate Mini Baking Bits, divided

Preheat oven to 350°F. Lightly grease 24 (2¾-inch) muffin cups or line with paper or foil liners. In large bowl combine flour, baking powder and salt. Blend in sugar, butter, milk and vanilla; beat 2 minutes. Add egg whites; beat 2 minutes. Divide batter evenly among prepared muffin cups. Place 2 drops desired food coloring into each muffin cup. Swirl gently with knife. Sprinkle evenly with ¾ cup "M&M's"® Chocolate Mini Baking Bits. Bake 20 to 25 minutes or until toothpick inserted in center comes out clean. Cool completely on wire racks. Combine frosting and blue food coloring. Spread frosting over cupcakes; decorate with remaining ¾ cup "M&M's"® Chocolate Mini Baking Bits to make rainbows. *Makes 24 cupcakes*

Red's Rockin'
Rainbow Cupcakes

Banana Split Cupcakes

1 (18.25 ounces) yellow cake mix, divided

1 cup water

1 cup mashed ripe bananas

3 eggs

1 cup chopped drained maraschino cherries

1½ cups miniature semi-sweet chocolate chips, divided

1½ cups prepared vanilla frosting

1 cup marshmallow creme

1 teaspoon shortening

30 whole maraschino cherries, drained and patted dry

1. Preheat oven to 350°F. Line 30 regular-size (2½-inch) muffin cups with paper muffin cup liners.

2. Reserve 2 tablespoons cake mix. Combine remaining cake mix, water, bananas and eggs in large bowl. Beat at low speed of electric mixer until moistened, about 30 seconds. Beat at medium speed 2 minutes. Combine chopped cherries and reserved cake mix in small bowl. Stir chopped cherry mixture and 1 cup chocolate chips into batter.

3. Spoon batter into prepared muffin cups. Bake 15 to 20 minutes or until toothpick inserted into centers comes out clean. Cool in pans on wire racks 10 minutes. Remove to wire racks; cool completely.

4. Combine frosting and marshmallow creme in medium bowl until well blended. Frost each cupcake with frosting mixture.

continued on page 120

Banana Split Cupcakes

Banana Split Cupcakes, continued

5. Combine remaining ½ cup chocolate chips and shortening in small microwavable bowl. Microwave at HIGH 30 to 45 seconds, stirring after 30 seconds, or until smooth. Drizzle chocolate mixture over cupcakes. Place one whole cherry on each cupcake.

Makes 30 cupcakes

Triple-Chocolate Cupcakes

- 1 package (18.25 ounces) chocolate cake mix
- 1 package (4 ounces) chocolate instant pudding and pie filling mix
- 1 container (8 ounces) sour cream
- 4 large eggs
- ½ cup vegetable oil
- ½ cup warm water
- 2 cups (12-ounce package) NESTLÉ® TOLL HOUSE® Semi-Sweet Chocolate Morsels
- 2 containers (16 ounces *each*) prepared frosting
  Assorted candy sprinkles

PREHEAT oven to 350°F. Grease or paper-line 30 muffin cups.

COMBINE cake mix, pudding mix, sour cream, eggs, vegetable oil and water in large mixer bowl; beat on low speed just until blended. Beat on high speed for 2 minutes. Stir in morsels. Pour into prepared muffin cups, filling ⅔ full.

BAKE for 25 to 28 minutes or until wooden pick inserted in center comes out clean. Cool in pans for 10 minutes; remove to wire racks to cool completely. Frost; decorate with candy sprinkles. *Makes about 30 cupcakes*

Brunchtime Sour Cream Cupcakes

1 cup (2 sticks) butter, softened

2 cups plus 4 teaspoons sugar, divided

2 eggs

1 cup sour cream

1 teaspoon almond extract

2 cups all-purpose flour

1 teaspoon salt

½ teaspoon baking soda

1 cup chopped walnuts

1½ teaspoons ground cinnamon

⅛ teaspoon nutmeg

1. Preheat oven to 350°F. Insert paper liners into 18 muffin cups. Beat butter and 2 cups sugar in large bowl. Add eggs, one at a time, beating well after each addition. Blend in sour cream and almond extract.

2. Combine flour, salt and baking soda in medium bowl. Add to butter mixture; mix well. Combine remaining 4 teaspoons sugar, walnuts, cinnamon and nutmeg in small bowl. Fill prepared muffin cups ⅓ full with batter; sprinkle with ⅔ of the walnut mixture.

3. Cover with remaining batter; sprinkle with remaining walnut mixture. Bake 25 to 30 minutes or until toothpick inserted into centers comes out clean. Remove cupcakes from pan; cool on wire rack.   *Makes 1½ dozen cupcakes*

Cappuccino Cupcakes

1 package (18.25 ounces) dark chocolate cake mix

1⅓ cups strong brewed or instant coffee at room
   temperature

⅓ cup vegetable oil or melted butter

3 large eggs

1 container (16 ounces) prepared vanilla frosting

2 tablespoons coffee liqueur

   Grated chocolate*

   Chocolate-covered coffee beans (optional)

   Additional coffee liqueur (optional)

*Grate half of a 3- or 4-ounce milk, dark chocolate or espresso chocolate candy
bar on the large holes of a standing grater.

1. Preheat oven to 350°F. Line 24 regular-size (2½-inch)
muffin cups with paper muffin cup liners.

2. Beat cake mix, coffee, oil and eggs with electric mixer
at low speed 30 seconds. Beat at medium speed 2 minutes.

3. Spoon batter into prepared muffin cups filling ⅔ full.
Bake 18 to 20 minutes or until toothpick inserted into
centers comes out clean. Cool in pans on wire racks
10 minutes. Remove from pans; cool completely.

4. Combine frosting and 2 tablespoons liqueur in small
bowl; mix well. Before frosting, poke about 10 holes in
cupcake with toothpick. Pour 1 to 2 teaspoons liqueur
over top of each cupcake, if desired. Frost and sprinkle
with chocolate. Garnish with chocolate-covered coffee
beans, if desired.   *Makes 24 cupcakes*

Cappuccino Cupcakes

Chocolate Peanut Butter Cups

1 package DUNCAN HINES® Moist Deluxe®
   Swiss Chocolate Cake Mix

1 container DUNCAN HINES® Creamy Home-
   Style Classic Vanilla Frosting

½ cup creamy peanut butter

15 miniature peanut butter cup candies, wrappers
   removed, cut in half vertically

1. Preheat oven to 350°F. Place 30 (2½-inch) paper liners in muffin cups.

2. Prepare, bake and cool cupcakes following package directions for basic recipe.

3. Combine vanilla frosting and peanut butter in medium bowl. Stir until smooth. Frost one cupcake. Decorate with peanut butter cup candy, cut-side down. Repeat with remaining cupcakes, frosting and candies.

Makes 30 servings

Tip: You may substitute Duncan Hines® Moist Deluxe® Devil's Food, Dark Chocolate Fudge or Butter Recipe Fudge Cake Mix flavors for Swiss Chocolate Cake Mix.

Chocolate Peanut Butter
Cups

Tempting Breakfast Treats

Pumpkin Bread

1 package (about 18 ounces) yellow cake mix
1 can (16 ounces) solid pack pumpkin
4 eggs
⅓ cup GRANDMA'S® Molasses
1 teaspoon cinnamon
1 teaspoon nutmeg
⅓ cup nuts, chopped (optional)
⅓ cup raisins (optional)

Preheat oven to 350°F. Grease two 9×5-inch loaf pans.

Combine all ingredients in large bowl and mix well. Beat at medium speed 2 minutes. Pour into prepared pans. Bake 60 minutes or until toothpick inserted into center comes out clean.   *Makes 2 loaves*

Hint: Serve with cream cheese or preserves, or top with cream cheese frosting or ice cream.

Pumpkin Bread

Peanut Butter Mini Muffins

⅓ cup creamy peanut butter

¼ cup (½ stick) butter, softened

¼ cup granulated sugar

¼ cup firmly packed light brown sugar

1 large egg

¾ cup buttermilk

3 tablespoons vegetable oil

¾ teaspoon vanilla extract

1½ cups all-purpose flour

¾ teaspoon baking powder

½ teaspoon baking soda

½ teaspoon salt

1¼ cups "M&M's"® Milk Chocolate Mini Baking Bits, divided

Chocolate Glaze (page 130)

Preheat oven to 350°F. Lightly grease 36 (1¾-inch) mini muffin cups or line with paper or foil liners; set aside. In large bowl cream peanut butter, butter and sugars until light and fluffy; beat in egg. Beat in buttermilk, oil and vanilla. In medium bowl combine flour, baking powder, baking soda and salt; gradually blend into creamed mixture. Divide batter evenly among prepared muffin cups. Sprinkle batter evenly with ¾ cup "M&M's"® Milk Chocolate Mini Baking Bits. Bake 15 to 17 minutes or until toothpick inserted in centers comes out clean. Cool completely on wire racks. Prepare Chocolate Glaze. Place

continued on page 130

Peanut Butter Mini Muffins

Peanut Butter Mini Muffins, *continued*

glaze in resealable plastic sandwich bag; seal bag. Cut tiny piece off one corner of bag (not more than ⅛ inch). Drizzle glaze over muffins. Decorate with remaining ½ cup "M&M's"® Milk Chocolate Mini Baking Bits. Store in tightly covered container.   *Makes 3 dozen mini muffins*

Chocolate Glaze: In top of double boiler over hot water melt 2 (1-ounce) squares semi-sweet chocolate and 1 tablespoon butter. Stir until smooth; let cool slightly.

Banana-Nana Pecan Bread

        1 cup QUAKER® Oats (quick or old fashioned,
            uncooked)
    ½ cup chopped pecans
        3 tablespoons margarine or butter, melted
        2 tablespoons firmly packed brown sugar
        1 (14-ounce) package banana bread quick bread mix
        1 cup water
    ½ cup mashed ripe banana
        2 eggs, lightly beaten
        3 tablespoons vegetable oil

Heat oven to 375°F. Grease and flour bottom only of 9×5-inch loaf pan. Combine oats, pecans, margarine and sugar; mix well. Reserve ½ cup oat mixture for topping; set aside. In bowl, combine remaining oat mixture, quick bread mix, water, banana, eggs and oil. Mix just until dry ingredients are moistened. Pour into prepared pan. Sprinkle top of loaf with reserved oat mixture. Bake 50 to 55 minutes or until wooden pick inserted in center comes out clean. Cool 10 minutes in pan; remove to wire rack. Cool.   *Makes 12 servings*

Cherry and Almond Coffee Cake

1 sheet (½ of 17¼-ounce package) frozen puff pastry
1 package (3 ounces) cream cheese, softened
⅓ cup plus 2 tablespoons powdered sugar, divided
1 egg, separated
¼ teaspoon almond extract
1 tablespoon water
½ cup dried cherries or cranberries, coarsely chopped
½ cup sliced almonds, divided

1. Thaw pastry sheet according to package directions.

2. Preheat oven to 375°F. Spray baking sheet with nonstick cooking spray. Combine cream cheese, ⅓ cup powdered sugar, egg yolk and almond extract in large bowl. Beat with electric mixer at medium speed until smooth. Mix egg white and water in separate small bowl.

3. Roll out pastry on lightly floured surface into 14×10-inch rectangle. Spread cream cheese mixture over dough, leaving 1-inch border. Sprinkle evenly with cherries. Reserve 2 tablespoons almonds; sprinkle remaining almonds over cherries.

4. Starting with long side, loosely roll up dough jelly-roll style. Place roll on baking sheet, seam side down. Form into circle, pinching ends together. Using scissors, cut at 1-inch intervals from outside of ring toward (but not through) center. Twist each section half a turn, allowing filling to show.

5. Brush top of ring with egg white mixture. Sprinkle with reserved almonds. Bake 25 to 30 minutes or until light brown. Carefully remove ring to wire rack. Cool 15 minutes; sprinkle with remaining 2 tablespoons powdered sugar. *Makes 1 (12-inch) coffee cake*

Blueberry Orange Muffins

1¾ cups all-purpose flour

⅓ cup sugar

2½ teaspoons baking powder

½ teaspoon baking soda

½ teaspoon salt

½ teaspoon ground cinnamon

¾ cup fat-free (skim) milk

1 egg, lightly beaten

¼ cup butter, melted and slightly cooled

3 tablespoons orange juice concentrate, thawed

1 teaspoon vanilla

¾ cup fresh or frozen blueberries, thawed

Preheat oven to 400°F. Grease muffin pan or line with paper baking cups.

Combine flour, sugar, baking powder, baking soda, salt and cinnamon in large bowl. Beat milk, egg, butter, orange juice concentrate and vanilla in medium bowl on medium speed of electric mixer until well combined. Add milk mixture to dry ingredients. Mix just until dry ingredients are barely moistened (mixture will be lumpy). Add berries; stir gently just until berries are evenly distributed.

Fill muffin cups ¾ full. Bake 20 to 25 minutes (25 to 30 minutes if using frozen berries) or until toothpick inserted into centers comes out clean. Let cool 5 minutes in pan. Remove to wire rack; serve warm.

Makes 12 muffins

Blueberry Orange Muffins

Lots o' Chocolate Bread

⅔ cup packed light brown sugar

½ cup butter, softened

1½ cups miniature semi-sweet chocolate chips, divided

2 eggs

2½ cups all-purpose flour

1½ cups applesauce

1½ teaspoons vanilla

1 teaspoon baking soda

1 teaspoon baking powder

½ teaspoon salt

½ cup chocolate chips

1 tablespoon shortening (do not use butter, margarine, spread or oil)

Preheat oven to 350°F. Grease 5 (5½×3-inch) mini loaf pans. Beat brown sugar and butter in large bowl with electric mixer until creamy. Melt 1 cup miniature chocolate chips; cool slightly and add to sugar mixture with eggs. Add flour, applesauce, vanilla, baking soda, baking powder and salt; beat until well mixed. Stir in remaining ½ cup miniature chocolate chips. Spoon batter into prepared pans; bake 35 to 40 minutes or until center cracks and is dry to the touch. Cool 10 minutes before removing from pans.

Place ½ cup chocolate chips and shortening in small microwavable bowl. Microwave at HIGH 1 minute; stir. If necessary, microwave at HIGH an additional 15 seconds at a time, stirring after each heating. Drizzle warm loaves with glaze. Cool completely.   *Makes 5 mini loaves*

Lots o' Chocolate Bread

Orange Streusel Coffeecake

Cocoa Streusel (page 138)
¾ cup (1½ sticks) butter or margarine, softened
1 cup sugar
3 eggs
1 teaspoon vanilla extract
½ cup dairy sour cream
3 cups all-purpose flour
2 teaspoons baking powder
1 teaspoon baking soda
1 cup orange juice
2 teaspoons freshly grated orange peel
½ cup orange marmalade or apple jelly

1. Prepare Cocoa Streusel. Heat oven to 350°F. Generously grease 12-cup fluted tube pan.

2. Beat butter and sugar in large bowl until well blended. Add eggs and vanilla; beat well. Add sour cream; beat until blended. Stir together flour, baking powder and baking soda; add alternately with orange juice to butter mixture, beating until well blended. Stir in orange peel.

3. Spread marmalade in bottom of prepared pan; sprinkle half of streusel over marmalade. Pour half of batter into pan, spreading evenly. Sprinkle remaining streusel over batter; spread remaining batter evenly over streusel.

4. Bake about 1 hour or until toothpick inserted near center comes out clean. Loosen cake from side of pan; immediately invert onto plate.   *Makes 12 servings*

continued on page 138

Orange Streusel Coffeecake

Orange Streusel Coffeecake, continued

Cocoa Streusel: Stir together ⅔ cup packed light brown sugar, ½ cup chopped walnuts, ¼ cup HERSHEY'S Cocoa and ½ cup MOUNDS® Sweetened Coconut Flakes, if desired.

Carrot and Raisin Muffins

- 2 cups all-purpose flour
- 1 tablespoon baking powder
- ½ teaspoon ground allspice (optional)
- ¼ teaspoon salt
- ¾ cup firmly packed dark brown sugar
- ½ cup (1 stick) SHEDD'S® Spread Country Crock Spread-Sticks
- 2 eggs
- 1 cup milk
- 1 cup raisins
- 1 carrot, shredded (about ¾ cup)

Preheat oven to 375°F. Grease 12-cup muffin pan or line with paper cupcake liners; set aside. In large bowl, combine flour, baking powder, allspice and salt; set aside.

In another large bowl, with electric mixer, beat sugar and SHEDD'S® Spread Country Crock Spread on medium-high speed until light and fluffy, about 5 minutes. Beat in eggs, scraping side occasionally, until blended. Alternately beat in flour mixture and milk until blended. Stir in raisins and carrot. Evenly spoon batter into prepared pan.

Bake 18 minutes or until toothpick inserted in centers comes out clean. On wire rack, cool 10 minutes; remove from pan and cool completely. *Makes 12 muffins*

Butterscotch Sticky Buns

3 tablespoons butter or margarine, *divided*

2 packages (8 ounces *each*) refrigerated crescent dinner rolls

1⅔ cups (11-ounce package) NESTLÉ® TOLL HOUSE® Butterscotch Flavored Morsels, *divided*

½ cup chopped pecans

¼ cup granulated sugar

1½ teaspoons lemon juice

1½ teaspoons water

1 teaspoon ground cinnamon

PREHEAT oven to 375°F.

PLACE *1 tablespoon* butter in 13×9-inch baking pan; melt in oven for 2 to 4 minutes or until butter sizzles. Unroll dinner rolls; separate into 16 triangles. Sprinkle triangles with 1⅓ *cups* morsels. Starting at shortest side, roll up each triangle; arrange in prepared baking pan.

BAKE for 15 to 20 minutes or until lightly browned.

MICROWAVE *remaining* morsels and *remaining* butter in medium, microwave-safe bowl on MEDIUM-HIGH (70%) power for 30 seconds; stir. Microwave at additional 10- to 20-second intervals, stirring until smooth. Stir in nuts, sugar, lemon juice, water and cinnamon. Pour over hot rolls.

BAKE for 5 minutes or until bubbly. Immediately loosen buns from pan. Cool in pan on wire rack for 10 minutes; serve warm. *Makes 16 buns*

Tropical Carrot Bread

Bread
- ⅓ CRISCO® Stick or ⅓ cup CRISCO® all-vegetable shortening plus additional for greasing
- ¾ cup firmly packed brown sugar
- 4 egg whites, lightly beaten
- 2¼ cups all-purpose flour
- 1 tablespoon plus 2 teaspoons baking powder
- ¾ teaspoon ground cinnamon
- ¼ teaspoon ground ginger
- ¼ teaspoon salt (optional)
- 1¼ cups uncooked old-fashioned or quick oats
- 1 cup shredded carrots
- 1 can (8 ounces) crushed pineapple in unsweetened juice
- ½ cup raisins

Topping
- 2 tablespoons uncooked old-fashioned or quick oats

1. Heat oven to 350°F. Grease 9×5×3-inch loaf pan.

2. For bread, combine shortening and brown sugar in large bowl. Beat at medium speed with electric mixer or stir with fork until well blended. Stir in egg whites. Beat until fairly smooth.

3. Combine flour, baking powder, cinnamon, ginger and salt in medium bowl. Stir into egg mixture. Stir in oats.

continued on page 142

Tropical Carrot Bread

Tropical Carrot Bread, *continued*

Add carrots and pineapple with juice. Stir until just blended. Stir in raisins. Spoon into prepared pan.

4. For topping, sprinkle oats evenly over batter.

5. Bake at 350°F for 70 to 80 minutes or until toothpick inserted in center comes out clean. Cool 10 minutes in pan on cooling rack. Loosen from sides. Remove from pan. Cool completely on cooling rack.

Makes 1 loaf (12 servings)

Kitchen Hint: A loaf of homemade bread makes a great gift—especially when it's given in a new loaf pan. Just add a wooden spoon and the recipe, wrap it all up in a festive towel and tie it with ribbon.

Gingerbread Streusel Raisin Muffins

1 cup raisins
½ cup boiling water
⅓ cup margarine or butter, softened
¾ cup GRANDMA'S® Molasses (Unsulphured)
1 egg
2 cups all-purpose flour
1½ teaspoons baking soda
1 teaspoon cinnamon
1 teaspoon ginger
½ teaspoon salt

Topping
⅓ cup all-purpose flour
¼ cup firmly packed brown sugar
¼ cup chopped nuts
3 tablespoons margarine or butter
1 teaspoon cinnamon

Preheat oven to 375°F. Grease bottoms only of 12 muffin
cups or line with paper baking cups. In small bowl, cover
raisins with boiling water; let stand 5 minutes. In large
bowl, beat ⅓ cup margarine and molasses until fluffy.
Add egg; beat well. Stir in 2 cups flour, baking soda,
1 teaspoon cinnamon, ginger and salt. Blend just until dry
ingredients are moistened. Gently stir in raisins and water.
Fill prepared muffin cups ¾ full. For topping, combine all
ingredients in small bowl. Sprinkle over muffins.

Bake 20 to 25 minutes or until toothpick inserted in
centers comes out clean. Cool 5 minutes; remove from
pan. Serve warm. *Makes 12 muffins*

Cranberry Streusel Coffee Cake

1 egg
½ cup plus 3 tablespoons sugar, divided
½ cup milk
1 tablespoon vegetable oil
1 tablespoon orange juice
1 teaspoon grated orange peel
¼ teaspoon almond extract
1½ cups all-purpose flour, divided
2 teaspoons baking powder
½ teaspoon salt
8 ounces (2 cups) fresh cranberries
2 tablespoons butter

1. Preheat oven to 375°F.

2. Beat egg in large bowl. Add ½ cup sugar, milk, oil, orange juice, orange peel and almond extract; mix thoroughly. Combine 1 cup flour, baking powder and salt; add to egg mixture and stir, being careful not to overmix. Pour into 8×8×2-inch pan sprayed with nonstick cooking spray.

3. Chop cranberries in blender or food processor; spoon over batter. Mix remaining ½ cup flour and remaining 3 tablespoons sugar. Cut in butter. Sprinkle mixture over cranberries.

4. Bake 25 to 30 minutes. Serve warm.

Makes 9 servings

Cranberry Streusel
Coffee Cake

White Chocolate Chunk Muffins

2½ cups all-purpose flour

1 cup packed brown sugar

⅓ cup unsweetened cocoa powder

2 teaspoons baking soda

½ teaspoon salt

1⅓ cups buttermilk

6 tablespoons butter, melted

2 eggs, beaten

1½ teaspoons vanilla

1½ cups chopped white chocolate

Preheat oven to 400°F. Grease 12 (3½-inch) large muffin cups; set aside.

Combine flour, sugar, cocoa, baking soda and salt in large bowl. Combine buttermilk, butter, eggs and vanilla in small bowl until blended. Stir into flour mixture just until moistened. Fold in white chocolate. Spoon into prepared muffin cups, filling half full.

Bake 25 to 30 minutes or until wooden pick inserted into centers comes out clean. Cool in pan on wire rack 5 minutes. Remove from pan. Cool on wire rack 10 minutes. Serve warm or cool completely.

Makes 12 jumbo muffins

White Chocolate
Chunk Muffins

Blueberry Kuchen

1½ cups all-purpose flour

2 teaspoons baking powder

½ cup EGG BEATERS® Healthy Real Egg Product

⅓ cup skim milk

1 teaspoon vanilla extract

½ cup granulated sugar

¼ cup FLEISCHMANN'S® Original Margarine, softened

1 (21-ounce) can blueberry pie filling and topping

Streusel Topping (page 150)

Powdered Sugar Glaze, optional (page 150)

In small bowl, combine flour and baking powder; set aside. In another small bowl, combine Egg Beaters®, milk and vanilla; set aside.

In medium bowl, with electric mixer at medium speed, beat granulated sugar and margarine until creamy. Alternately add flour mixture and egg mixture, blending well after each addition. Spread batter into greased 9-inch square baking pan.

Bake at 350°F for 20 minutes. Spoon blueberry pie filling over batter; sprinkle Streusel Topping over filling. Bake for 10 to 15 minutes more or until toothpick inserted in center comes out clean. Cool in pan on wire rack. Drizzle with Powdered Sugar Glaze, if desired. Cut into 12 (3×2-inch) pieces.   *Makes 12 servings*

continued on page 150

Blueberry Kuchen

Blueberry Kuchen, *continued*

Streusel Topping: In small bowl, combine 3 tablespoons all-purpose flour, 3 tablespoons powdered sugar and ¼ teaspoon ground cinnamon. Cut in 1 tablespoon Fleischmann's Original Margarine until crumbly.

Powdered Sugar Glaze: In small bowl, combine 1 cup powdered sugar and 5 to 6 teaspoons water until smooth.

Prep Time: 20 minutes
Cook Time: 35 minutes

Cranberry Orange Ring

       2 cups all-purpose flour
       1 cup sugar
    1½ teaspoons baking powder
       1 teaspoon salt
     ½ teaspoon baking soda
     ¼ teaspoon ground cloves
       1 tablespoon minced orange peel
     ¾ cup orange juice
       1 egg, lightly beaten
       2 tablespoons vegetable oil
       1 teaspoon vanilla
     ¼ teaspoon orange extract
       1 cup whole cranberries

Preheat oven to 350°F. Grease 12-cup tube pan.

Combine flour, sugar, baking powder, salt, baking soda and cloves in large bowl. Add orange peel; mix well. Set aside. Combine orange juice, egg, oil, vanilla and orange extract in medium bowl. Beat until well blended. Add orange

Breakfast Treats

juice mixture to flour mixture. Stir until just moistened. Gently fold in cranberries. Do not overmix.

Spread batter in prepared pan. Bake 30 to 35 minutes (35 to 40 minutes if using frozen cranberries) or until toothpick inserted in center comes out clean. Cool in pan on wire rack 15 to 20 minutes. Invert onto serving plate. Serve warm or at room temperature.   *Makes 12 servings*

Lemon Poppy Seed Muffins

        3 cups all-purpose flour
        1 cup sugar
        3 tablespoons poppy seeds
        1 tablespoon grated lemon peel
        2 teaspoons baking powder
        1 teaspoon baking soda
    ½ teaspoon salt
        1 container (16 ounces) plain low-fat yogurt
    ½ cup fresh lemon juice
        2 eggs, beaten
    ¼ cup vegetable oil
    1½ teaspoons vanilla

Preheat oven to 400°F. Grease 12 (3½-inch) large muffin cups; set aside. Combine flour, sugar, poppy seeds, lemon peel, baking powder, baking soda and salt in large bowl. Combine yogurt, lemon juice, eggs, oil and vanilla in small bowl until well blended. Stir into flour mixture just until moistened. Spoon into prepared muffin cups, filling two-thirds full. Bake 25 to 30 minutes or until wooden pick inserted into centers comes out clean. Cool in pans on wire racks 5 minutes. Remove from pans. Cool on wire racks 10 minutes. Serve warm or cool completely.

Makes 12 jumbo muffins

Toll House Crumbcake

Topping
- ⅓ cup packed brown sugar
- 1 tablespoon all-purpose flour
- 2 tablespoons butter or margarine, softened
- ½ cup chopped nuts
- 2 cups (12-ounce package) NESTLÉ® TOLL HOUSE® Semi-Sweet Chocolate Mini Morsels, *divided*

Cake
- 1¾ cups all-purpose flour
- 1 teaspoon baking powder
- 1 teaspoon baking soda
- ¼ teaspoon salt
- ¾ cup granulated sugar
- ½ cup (1 stick) butter or margarine, softened
- 1 teaspoon vanilla extract
- 3 large eggs
- 1 cup sour cream

PREHEAT oven to 350°F. Grease 13×9-inch baking pan.

For Topping
COMBINE brown sugar, flour and butter in small bowl with pastry blender or two knives until crumbly. Stir in nuts and ½ *cup* morsels.

For Cake
COMBINE flour, baking powder, baking soda and salt. Beat granulated sugar, butter and vanilla extract in large mixer bowl until creamy. Add eggs, one at a time, beating

continued on page 154

Toll House Crumbcake

Toll House Crumbcake, *continued*

well after each addition. Gradually add flour mixture alternately with sour cream. Fold in *remaining* morsels. Spread into prepared baking pan; sprinkle with topping.

BAKE for 25 to 35 minutes or until wooden pick inserted in center comes out clean. Cool in pan on wire rack.

Makes 12 servings

Cranberry Oat Bread

¾ cup honey
⅓ cup vegetable oil
2 eggs
½ cup milk
2½ cups all-purpose flour
1 cup quick-cooking rolled oats
1 teaspoon baking soda
1 teaspoon baking powder
½ teaspoon salt
½ teaspoon ground cinnamon
2 cups fresh or frozen cranberries
1 cup chopped nuts

Combine honey, oil, eggs and milk in large bowl; mix well. Combine flour, oats, baking soda, baking powder, salt and cinnamon in medium bowl; mix well. Stir into honey mixture. Fold in cranberries and nuts. Spoon into two 8½×4½×2½-inch greased and floured loaf pans.

Bake in preheated 350°F oven 40 to 45 minutes or until wooden toothpick inserted near center comes out clean. Cool in pans on wire racks 15 minutes. Remove from pans; cool completely on wire racks.   *Makes 2 loaves*

Favorite recipe from **National Honey Board**

Fudgey Peanut Butter Chip Muffins

½ cup applesauce
½ cup quick-cooking rolled oats
¼ cup (½ stick) butter or margarine, softened
½ cup granulated sugar
½ cup packed light brown sugar
1 egg
½ teaspoon vanilla extract
¾ cup all-purpose flour
¼ cup HERSHEY'S Dutch Processed Cocoa
    or HERSHEY'S Cocoa
½ teaspoon baking soda
¼ teaspoon ground cinnamon (optional)
1 cup REESE'S® Peanut Butter Chips
Powdered sugar (optional)

1. Heat oven to 350°F. Line muffin cups (2½ inches in diameter) with paper bake cups.

2. Blend applesauce and oats in small bowl. Beat butter, granulated sugar, brown sugar, egg and vanilla in large bowl until well blended. Add applesauce mixture; blend well. Stir together flour, cocoa, baking soda and cinnamon, if desired. Add to butter mixture, blending well. Stir in peanut butter chips. Fill muffin cups ¾ full with batter.

3. Bake 22 to 26 minutes or until wooden pick inserted in center comes out almost clean. Cool slightly in pan on wire rack. Sprinkle muffin tops with powdered sugar, if desired. Serve warm.   *Makes 12 to 15 muffins*

Fudgey Chocolate Chip Muffins: Omit Peanut Butter Chips. Add 1 cup HERSHEY'S Semi-Sweet Chocolate Chips.

Tex-Mex Quick Bread

1½ cups all-purpose flour

1 cup (4 ounces) shredded Monterey Jack cheese

½ cup cornmeal

½ cup sun-dried tomatoes, coarsely chopped

1 can (4¼ ounces) black olives, drained and chopped

¼ cup sugar

1½ teaspoons baking powder

1 teaspoon baking soda

1 cup milk

1 can (4½ ounces) green chilies, drained and chopped

¼ cup olive oil

1 large egg, beaten

1. Preheat oven to 325°F. Grease 9×5-inch loaf pan or four 5×3-inch loaf pans; set aside.

2. Combine flour, cheese, cornmeal, tomatoes, olives, sugar, baking powder and baking soda in large bowl.

3. Combine remaining ingredients in small bowl. Add to flour mixture; stir just until combined. Pour into prepared pan. Bake 9×5-inch loaf 45 minutes and 5×3-inch loaves 30 minutes or until toothpick inserted into center of loaf comes out clean. Cool in pan 15 minutes. Remove from pan and cool on wire rack.

Makes 1 large loaf or 4 small loaves

Muffin Variation: Preheat oven to 375°F. Spoon batter into 12 well-greased muffin cups. Bake 20 minutes or until toothpick inserted into centers of muffins comes out clean. Makes 12 muffins.

Tex-Mex Quick Bread

Crowd-Pleasing Cakes

Orange Glazed Pound Cake

1 package DUNCAN HINES® Moist Deluxe®
    Butter Recipe Golden Cake Mix

4 eggs

1 cup sour cream

⅓ cup vegetable oil

¼ cup plus 1 to 2 tablespoons orange juice, divided

2 tablespoons grated orange peel

1 cup confectioners' sugar

1. Preheat oven to 375°F. Grease and flour 10-inch tube pan.

2. Combine cake mix, eggs, sour cream, oil, ¼ cup orange juice and orange peel in large bowl. Beat at medium speed with electric mixer for 2 minutes. Pour into prepared pan. Bake at 375°F for 45 to 50 minutes or until toothpick inserted in center comes out clean. Cool in pan 25 minutes. Invert onto cooling rack. Cool completely.

3. Combine sugar and remaining 1 to 2 tablespoons orange juice in small bowl; stir until smooth. Drizzle over cake. Garnish as desired.   *Makes 12 to 16 servings*

Orange Glazed Pound Cake

Choca-Cola Cake

Cake
  1¾ cups granulated sugar
   ¾ CRISCO® Stick or ¾ cup CRISCO® all-vegetable
      shortening
   2 eggs
   2 tablespoons cocoa
   1 tablespoon vanilla
   ¼ teaspoon salt
   ½ cup buttermilk or sour milk*
   1 teaspoon baking soda
  2½ cups all-purpose flour
   1 cup cola soft drink (not sugar-free)

Frosting
   1 box (1 pound) confectioners' sugar (3½ to 4 cups)
   6 tablespoons or more cola soft drink (not sugar-free)
   ¼ cup cocoa
   ¼ cup CRISCO® Stick or ¼ cup CRISCO®
      all-vegetable shortening
   1 cup chopped pecans, divided

*To sour milk: Combine 1½ teaspoons white vinegar plus enough milk to equal ½ cup. Stir. Wait 5 minutes before using.

1. Heat oven to 350°F. Line bottom of 13×9×2-inch baking pan with waxed paper.

2. For cake, combine granulated sugar and shortening in large bowl. Beat at medium speed of electric mixer

continued on page 162

Choca-Cola Cake

Choca-Cola Cake, *continued*

1 minute. Add eggs. Beat until blended. Add
2 tablespoons cocoa, vanilla and salt. Beat until blended.

3. Combine buttermilk and baking soda in small bowl.
Add to creamed mixture. Beat until blended. Reduce
speed to low. Add flour alternately with 1 cup cola,
beginning and ending with flour, beating at low speed
after each addition until well blended. Pour into pan.

4. Bake at 350°F for 30 to 35 minutes or until cake begins
to pull away from sides of pan. *Do not overbake.* Cool
10 minutes before removing from pan. Invert cake on
wire rack. Remove waxed paper. Cool completely. Place
cake on serving tray.

5. For frosting, combine confectioners' sugar,
6 tablespoons cola, ¼ cup cocoa and ¼ cup shortening
in medium bowl. Beat at low, then medium speed until
blended, adding more cola, if necessary, until of desired
spreading consistency. Stir in ½ cup nuts. Frost top and
sides of cake. Sprinkle remaining nuts over top of cake.
Let stand at least 1 hour before serving.

Makes 1 (13×9×2-inch) cake (12 to 16 servings)

Note: Flavor of cake improves if made several hours or a
day before serving.

Southern Jam Cake

Cake
- ¾ cup butter or margarine, softened
- 1 cup granulated sugar
- 3 eggs
- 1 cup (12-ounce jar) SMUCKER'S® Seedless Blackberry Jam
- 2½ cups all-purpose flour
- 1 teaspoon baking soda
- 1 teaspoon ground cinnamon
- 1 teaspoon ground cloves
- 1 teaspoon ground allspice
- 1 teaspoon ground nutmeg
- ¾ cup buttermilk

Caramel Icing (optional)
- 2 tablespoons butter
- ½ cup firmly packed brown sugar
- 3 tablespoons milk
- 1¾ cups powdered sugar

Grease and flour tube pan. Combine ¾ cup butter and granulated sugar; beat until light and fluffy. Add eggs one at a time, beating well after each addition. Fold in jam.

Combine flour, baking soda and spices; mix well. Add to batter alternately with buttermilk, stirring just to blend after each addition. Spoon mixture into prepared pan.

Bake at 350°F for 50 minutes or until toothpick inserted in center comes out clean. Cool in pan for 10 minutes. Remove from pan; cool completely. In saucepan, melt 2 tablespoons butter; stir in brown sugar. Cook, stirring constantly, until mixture boils; remove from heat. Cool 5 minutes. Stir in milk; blend in powdered sugar. Frost cake.   *Makes 12 to 16 servings*

Carrot Layer Cake

Cake
- 1 package DUNCAN HINES® Moist Deluxe® Classic Yellow Cake Mix
- 4 eggs
- ½ cup vegetable oil
- 3 cups grated carrots
- 1 cup finely chopped nuts
- 2 teaspoons ground cinnamon

Cream Cheese Frosting
- 1 package (8 ounces) cream cheese, softened
- ¼ cup butter or margarine, softened
- 2 teaspoons vanilla extract
- 4 cups confectioners' sugar

1. Preheat oven to 350°F. Grease and flour two 8- or 9-inch round baking pans.

2. For cake, combine cake mix, eggs, oil, carrots, nuts and cinnamon in large bowl. Beat at low speed with electric mixer until moistened. Beat at medium speed for 2 minutes. Pour into prepared pans. Bake at 350°F for 35 to 40 minutes or until toothpick inserted in centers comes out clean. Cool.

3. For cream cheese frosting, place cream cheese, butter and vanilla extract in large bowl. Beat at low speed until smooth and creamy. Add confectioners' sugar gradually, beating until smooth. Add more sugar to thicken, or milk or water to thin frosting, as needed. Fill and frost cooled cake. Garnish with whole pecans.

Makes 12 to 16 servings

Carrot Layer Cake

Strawberry Stripe Refrigerator Cake

Cake
- 1 package DUNCAN HINES® Moist Deluxe® Classic White Cake Mix
- 2 packages (10 ounces) frozen sweetened strawberry slices, thawed

Topping
- 1 package (4-serving size) vanilla-flavor instant pudding and pie filling mix
- 1 cup milk
- 1 cup whipping cream, whipped
- Fresh strawberries for garnish (optional)

1. Preheat oven to 350°F. Grease and flour 13×9×2-inch baking pan.

2. For cake, prepare, bake and cool following package directions. Poke holes 1 inch apart in top of cake using handle of wooden spoon. Purée thawed strawberries with juice in blender or food processor. Spoon evenly over top of cake, allowing mixture to soak into holes.

3. For topping, combine pudding mix and milk in large bowl. Stir until smooth. Fold in whipped cream. Spread over cake. Decorate with fresh strawberries, if desired. Refrigerate at least 4 hours. *Makes 12 to 16 servings*

Tip: For Neapolitan Cake, replace White Cake Mix with Duncan Hines® Moist Deluxe® Devil's Food Cake Mix.

Zesty Lemon Pound Cake

1 cup (6 ounces) NESTLÉ® TOLL HOUSE®
    Premier White Morsels or 3 bars (6-ounce box)
    NESTLÉ® TOLL HOUSE® Premier White
    Baking Bars, broken into pieces

2½ cups all-purpose flour

1 teaspoon baking powder

½ teaspoon salt

1 cup (2 sticks) butter, softened

1½ cups granulated sugar

2 teaspoons vanilla extract

3 large eggs

3 to 4 tablespoons (about 3 medium lemons) grated
    lemon peel

1⅓ cups buttermilk

1 cup powdered sugar

3 tablespoons fresh lemon juice

PREHEAT oven to 350°F. Grease and flour 12-cup
bundt pan.

MELT morsels in medium, microwave-safe bowl on
MEDIUM-HIGH (70%) power for 1 minute; stir.
Microwave at additional 10- to 20-second intervals,
stirring until smooth; cool slightly.

COMBINE flour, baking powder and salt in small bowl.
Beat butter, granulated sugar and vanilla extract in large
mixer bowl until creamy. Beat in eggs, one at a time,
beating well after each addition. Beat in lemon peel

continued on page 170

Zesty Lemon Pound Cake

Zesty Lemon Pound Cake, *continued*

and melted morsels. Gradually beat in flour mixture alternately with buttermilk. Pour into prepared bundt pan.

BAKE for 50 to 55 minutes or until wooden pick inserted in cake comes out clean. Cool in pan on wire rack for 10 minutes. Combine powdered sugar and lemon juice in small bowl. Make holes in cake with wooden pick; pour *half* of lemon glaze over cake. Let stand for 5 minutes. Invert onto plate. Make holes in top of cake; pour *remaining* glaze over cake. Cool completely before serving.   *Makes 16 servings*

Take-Along Cake

1 package DUNCAN HINES® Moist Deluxe® Swiss Chocolate Cake Mix

1 package (12 ounces) semisweet chocolate chips

1 cup miniature marshmallows

¼ cup butter or margarine, melted

½ cup packed brown sugar

½ cup chopped pecans or walnuts

1. Preheat oven to 350°F. Grease and flour 13×9-inch baking pan.

2. Prepare cake mix as directed on package. Add chocolate chips and marshmallows to batter. Pour into prepared pan. Drizzle melted butter over batter. Sprinkle with sugar and top with pecans. Bake at 350°F for 45 to 55 minutes or until toothpick inserted in center comes out clean. Serve warm or cool completely in pan.

Makes 12 to 16 servings

Tip: To keep leftover pecans fresh, store them in the freezer in an airtight container.

Pumpkin Pecan Rum Cake

¾ cup chopped pecans
3 cups all-purpose flour
2 tablespoons pumpkin pie spice
2 teaspoons baking soda
1 teaspoon salt
1 cup (2 sticks) butter or margarine, softened
1 cup packed brown sugar
1 cup granulated sugar
4 large eggs
1 can (15 ounces) LIBBY'S® 100% Pure Pumpkin
1 teaspoon vanilla extract
Rum Butter Glaze (recipe follows)

PREHEAT oven to 325°F. Grease 12-cup bundt pan. Sprinkle nuts over bottom.

COMBINE flour, pumpkin pie spice, baking soda and salt in medium bowl. Beat butter, brown sugar and granulated sugar in large mixer bowl until light and fluffy. Add eggs; beat well. Add pumpkin and vanilla extract; beat well. Add flour mixture to pumpkin mixture, ⅓ at a time, mixing well after each addition. Spoon batter into prepared pan.

BAKE for 60 to 70 minutes or until wooden pick comes out clean. Cool 10 minutes. Make holes in cake with long pick; pour *half* of glaze over cake. Let stand 5 minutes and invert onto plate. Make holes in top of cake; pour *remaining* glaze over cake. Cool.   *Makes 24 servings*

Rum Butter Glaze: MELT ¼ cup butter or margarine in small saucepan; stir in ½ cup granulated sugar and 2 tablespoons water. Bring to a boil. Remove from heat; stir in 2 to 3 tablespoons dark rum or 1 teaspoon rum extract.

Hershey's Red Velvet Cake

½ cup (1 stick) butter or margarine, softened

1½ cups sugar

2 eggs

1 teaspoon vanilla extract

1 cup buttermilk or sour milk*

2 tablespoons (1-ounce bottle) red food color

2 cups all-purpose flour

⅓ cup HERSHEY'S Cocoa

1 teaspoon salt

1½ teaspoons baking soda

1 tablespoon white vinegar

1 can (16 ounces) ready-to-spread vanilla frosting

HERSHEY'S MINI CHIPS™ Semi-Sweet
Chocolate Chips or HERSHEY'S Milk
Chocolate Chips (optional)

To sour milk: Use 1 tablespoon white vinegar plus milk to equal 1 cup.

1. Heat oven to 350°F. Grease and flour 13×9×2-inch baking pan.

2. Beat butter and sugar in large bowl; add eggs and vanilla, beating well. Stir together buttermilk and food color. Stir together flour, cocoa and salt; add alternately to butter mixture with buttermilk mixture, mixing well. Stir in baking soda and vinegar. Pour into prepared pan.

3. Bake 30 to 35 minutes or until wooden pick inserted in center comes out clean. Cool completely in pan on wire rack. Frost; garnish with chocolate chips, if desired.

Makes about 15 servings

Hershey's Red Velvet Cake

Lemon Crumb Cake

1 package **DUNCAN HINES® Moist Deluxe®
Lemon Supreme Cake Mix**

3 **eggs**

1⅓ **cups water**

⅓ **cup vegetable oil**

1 **cup all-purpose flour**

½ **cup packed light brown sugar**

½ **teaspoon baking powder**

½ **cup butter or margarine**

1. Preheat oven to 350°F. Grease and flour 13×9-inch baking pan.

2. Combine cake mix, eggs, water and oil in large mixing bowl. Beat at medium speed with electric mixer for 2 minutes. Pour into prepared pan. Combine flour, sugar and baking powder in small bowl. Cut in butter until crumbly. Sprinkle evenly over batter. Bake at 350°F for 35 to 40 minutes or until toothpick inserted in center comes out clean. Cool completely in pan.

Makes 12 to 16 servings

Tip: Butter or margarine will cut more easily into the flour mixture if it is chilled. Use two knives or a pastry cutter to cut the mixture into crumbs.

Lemon Crumb Cake

Glazed Chocolate Pound Cake

Cake

1¾ Butter Flavor CRISCO® Sticks or 1¾ cups Butter
     Flavor CRISCO® all-vegetable shortening
     plus additional for greasing

3 cups granulated sugar

5 eggs

1 teaspoon vanilla

3¼ cups all-purpose flour

½ cup unsweetened cocoa powder

1 teaspoon baking powder

½ teaspoon salt

1⅓ cups milk

1 cup miniature semisweet chocolate chips

Glaze

1 cup miniature semisweet chocolate chips

¼ Butter Flavor CRISCO® Stick or ¼ cup Butter
     Flavor CRISCO® all-vegetable shortening

1 tablespoon light corn syrup

1. For cake, heat oven to 325°F. Grease and flour 10-inch tube pan.

2. Combine 1¾ cups shortening, sugar, eggs and vanilla in large bowl. Beat at low speed with electric mixer until blended, scraping bowl frequently. Beat at high speed 6 minutes, scraping bowl occasionally. Combine flour,

continued on page 178

Glazed Chocolate
Pound Cake

Glazed Chocolate Pound Cake, *continued*

cocoa, baking powder and salt in medium bowl. Mix in dry ingredients alternately with milk, beating after each addition until batter is smooth. Stir in 1 cup chocolate chips. Spoon into prepared pan.

3. Bake at 325°F for 75 to 85 minutes or until toothpick inserted near center comes out clean. Cool on cooling rack 20 minutes. Invert onto serving dish. Cool completely.

4. For glaze, combine 1 cup chocolate chips, ¼ cup shortening and corn syrup in top part of double boiler over hot, not boiling, water. Stir until just melted and smooth. Cool slightly. (Or place mixture in microwave-safe bowl. Microwave at 50% (Medium) power for 1 minute and 15 seconds. Stir. Repeat at 15-second intervals, if necessary, until just melted and smooth. Cool slightly.) Spoon glaze over cake. Let stand until glaze is firm.   *Makes 1 (10-inch) tube cake*

Prep Time: about 30 minutes
Bake Time: 75 to 85 minutes

Strawberry Pound Cake

1 package DUNCAN HINES® Moist Deluxe®
    Strawberry Supreme Cake Mix

1 package (4-serving size) vanilla-flavor instant
    pudding and pie filling mix

4 eggs

1 cup water

⅓ cup vegetable oil

1 cup mini semisweet chocolate chips

⅔ cup DUNCAN HINES® Creamy Home-Style
    Chocolate Buttercream Frosting

1. Preheat oven to 350°F. Grease and flour 10-inch
Bundt pan.

2. Combine cake mix, pudding mix, eggs, water and oil in
large mixing bowl. Beat at low speed with electric mixer
until moistened. Beat at medium speed for 2 minutes. Stir
in chocolate chips. Pour into prepared pan. Bake at 350°F
for 55 to 60 minutes or until toothpick inserted in center
comes out clean. Cool in pan 25 minutes. Invert onto
cooling rack. Cool completely.

3. Place frosting in 1-cup glass measuring cup. Microwave
at HIGH for 10 to 15 seconds. Stir until smooth. Drizzle
over top of cooled cake.   *Makes 12 to 16 servings*

Tip: Store leftover chocolate buttercream frosting,
covered, in refrigerator. Spread frosting between graham
crackers for a quick snack.

Brownie Apple Sauce Cake

½ cup butter
3 squares (1 ounce each) unsweetened chocolate
1½ cups MOTT'S® Apple Sauce
1 cup sugar
3 eggs, well beaten
1 teaspoon vanilla extract
1½ cups all-purpose flour
1 teaspoon baking soda
½ teaspoon salt
½ cup chopped walnuts
Apple Cream Cheese Frosting (recipe follows)

1. Heat oven to 350°F. In large heavy saucepan, over low heat, melt butter and chocolate, stirring constantly. Remove from heat and cool. Blend apple sauce, sugar, eggs and vanilla into chocolate mixture. In large bowl, mix flour, baking soda and salt. With wooden spoon, stir in chocolate mixture until blended. Stir in walnuts.

2. Pour batter into 2 greased and floured 8-inch round cake pans. Bake 35 to 40 minutes or until toothpick inserted in center comes out clean. Cool in pans 10 minutes. Prepare Apple Cream Cheese Frosting. Remove cakes from pans; cool completely on wire racks. Fill and frost with Apple Cream Cheese Frosting. Garnish as desired.   *Makes 12 servings*

Apple Cream Cheese Frosting: In large bowl, beat 2 packages (8 ounces each) softened cream cheese and

continued on page 182

Brownie Apple Sauce Cake

Brownie Apple Sauce Cake, continued

½ cup softened butter until light and fluffy. Blend in
1 cup confectioners' sugar, ½ cup MOTT'S® Apple Sauce,
½ cup melted and cooled caramels and 1 teaspoon vanilla
extract.

Orange Glow Bundt Cake

> 1 (18.25-ounce) package moist yellow cake mix
> 1 tablespoon grated orange peel
> 1 cup orange juice
> ¼ cup sugar
> 1 tablespoon TABASCO® brand Pepper Sauce
> 1¾ cups confectioners' sugar

Preheat oven to 375°F. Grease 12-cup Bundt pan. Prepare
cake mix according to package directions, adding orange
peel to batter. Bake 35 to 40 minutes or until toothpick
inserted in center of cake comes out clean.

Meanwhile, heat orange juice, sugar and TABASCO®
Sauce to boiling in 1-quart saucepan. Reduce heat to low;
simmer, uncovered, 5 minutes. Remove from heat.
Reserve ¼ cup orange juice mixture for glaze.

Remove cake from oven. With wooden skewer, poke
holes in cake (in pan) in several places. Spoon remaining
orange juice mixture over cake. Cool cake in pan
10 minutes. Carefully invert cake onto wire rack to
cool completely.

Combine reserved ¼ cup orange juice mixture and
confectioners' sugar in small bowl until smooth. Place
cake on platter; spoon glaze over cake. Garnish with
clusters of dried cranberries, mint leaves and grated
orange peel, if desired.   *Makes 12 servings*

Chocolate Sheet Cake

1¼ cups (2½ sticks) butter or margarine, divided

1 cup water

½ cup unsweetened cocoa, divided

2 cups all-purpose flour

1½ cups firmly packed light brown sugar

1 teaspoon baking soda

1 teaspoon ground cinnamon

½ teaspoon salt

1 (14-ounce) can EAGLE® BRAND Sweetened Condensed Milk (NOT evaporated milk), divided

2 eggs

1 teaspoon vanilla extract

1 cup powdered sugar

1 cup coarsely chopped nuts

1. Preheat oven to 350°F. In small saucepan over medium heat, melt 1 cup butter; stir in water and ¼ cup cocoa. Bring to a boil; remove from heat. In large mixing bowl, combine flour, brown sugar, baking soda, cinnamon and salt. Add cocoa mixture; beat well. Stir in ⅓ cup Eagle Brand, eggs and vanilla. Pour into greased 15×10×1-inch jelly-roll pan. Bake 15 minutes or until cake springs back when lightly touched.

2. In small saucepan over medium heat, melt remaining ¼ cup butter; add remaining ¼ cup cocoa and remaining Eagle Brand. Stir in powdered sugar and nuts. Spread over warm cake.   *Makes one 15×10-inch cake*

Rich & Gooey
Apple-Caramel Cake

Cake

      PAM® No-Stick Cooking Spray

  2 cups all-purpose flour

  1 teaspoon salt

  1 teaspoon baking soda

  1 teaspoon pumpkin pie spice

1½ cups sugar

  ¾ cup WESSON® Vegetable Oil

  3 eggs

  2 teaspoons vanilla

  3 cups peeled, cored and sliced tart apples,
      such as Granny Smith (½-inch slices)

  1 cup chopped walnuts

Glaze

  1 cup firmly packed light brown sugar

  ½ cup (1 stick) butter

  ¼ cup milk

  Whipped cream

For cake, preheat oven to 350°F. Spray 13×9×2-inch
baking pan with PAM® Cooking Spray; set aside. In
medium bowl, combine flour, salt, baking soda and pie
spice; mix well. Set aside. In large bowl, with electric
mixer, beat sugar, Wesson® Oil, eggs and vanilla for
3 minutes at medium speed. Add flour mixture and stir

continued on page 186

**Rich & Gooey
Apple-Caramel Cake**

Rich & Gooey Apple-Caramel Cake, continued

until dry ingredients are moistened; fold in apples and walnuts. Pour batter into baking pan and spread evenly; bake 50 to 55 minutes or until wooden pick inserted into center comes out clean. Cool cake in pan on wire rack.

Meanwhile, for glaze, in small saucepan over medium heat, bring brown sugar, butter and milk to a boil, stirring until sugar has dissolved. Boil 1 minute. Spoon half of glaze over warm cake; set *remaining* aside. Allow cake to stand 5 minutes. Top *each* serving with *remaining* glaze and whipped cream.   *Makes 12 to 15 servings*

Hershey's "Perfectly Chocolate" Chocolate Cake

2 cups sugar

1¾ cups all-purpose flour

¾ cup HERSHEY'S Cocoa or HERSHEY'S Dutch Processed Cocoa

1½ teaspoons baking powder

1½ teaspoons baking soda

1 teaspoon salt

2 eggs

1 cup milk

½ cup vegetable oil

2 teaspoons vanilla extract

1 cup boiling water

"Perfectly Chocolate" Chocolate Frosting (recipe follows)

1. Heat oven to 350°F. Grease and flour two 9-inch round baking pans.*

186

2. Stir together sugar, flour, cocoa, baking powder, baking soda and salt in large bowl. Add eggs, milk, oil and vanilla; beat on medium speed of mixer 2 minutes. Stir in water. (Batter will be thin.) Pour batter evenly into prepared pans.

3. Bake 30 to 35 minutes or until wooden pick inserted in center comes out clean. Cool 10 minutes; remove from pans to wire racks. Cool completely.

4. Prepare "Perfectly Chocolate" Chocolate Frosting; spread between layers and over top and sides of cake.

Makes 8 to 10 servings

One 13×9×2-inch baking pan may be substituted for 9-inch round baking pans. Prepare as directed above. Bake 35 to 40 minutes. Cool completely in pan on wire rack. Frost as desired.

"Perfectly Chocolate" Chocolate Frosting

1 stick (½ cup) butter or margarine
⅔ cup HERSHEY'S Cocoa
3 cups powdered sugar
⅓ cup milk
1 teaspoon vanilla extract

1. Melt butter. Stir in cocoa. Alternately add powdered sugar and milk, beating to spreading consistency.

2. Add small amount additional milk, if needed. Stir in vanilla.

Makes about 2 cups frosting

Banana Fudge Layer Cake

1 package DUNCAN HINES® Moist Deluxe®
    Yellow Cake Mix
1⅓ cups water
3 eggs
⅓ cup vegetable oil
1 cup mashed ripe bananas (about 3 medium)
1 container DUNCAN HINES® Chocolate Frosting

1. Preheat oven to 350°F. Grease and flour two 9-inch round cake pans.

2. Combine cake mix, water, eggs and oil in large bowl. Beat at low speed with electric mixer until moistened. Beat at medium speed 2 minutes. Stir in bananas.

3. Pour into prepared pans. Bake at 350°F for 28 to 31 minutes or until toothpick inserted in center comes out clean. Cool in pans 15 minutes. Remove from pans; cool completely.

4. Fill and frost cake with frosting. Garnish as desired.

Makes 12 to 16 servings

Perfect Pies

Orange Pecan Pie

3 eggs

½ cup GRANDMA'S® Molasses

½ cup light corn syrup

¼ cup orange juice

1 teaspoon grated orange peel

1 teaspoon vanilla

1½ cups whole pecan halves

1 (9-inch) unbaked pie shell

Whipping cream (optional)

Heat oven to 350°F. In large bowl, beat eggs. Add molasses, corn syrup, orange juice, orange peel and vanilla; beat until well blended. Stir in pecans. Pour into unbaked pie shell. Bake 30 to 45 minutes or until filling sets. Cool on wire rack. Serve with whipping cream, if desired.

Makes 8 servings

Orange Pecan Pie

Very Cherry Pie

4 cups frozen unsweetened tart cherries
1 cup dried tart cherries
1 cup sugar
2 tablespoons quick-cooking tapioca
½ teaspoon almond extract
    Pastry for double-crust 9-inch pie
¼ teaspoon ground nutmeg
1 tablespoon butter

Combine frozen cherries, dried cherries, sugar, tapioca and almond extract in large mixing bowl; mix well. (It is not necessary to thaw cherries before using.) Let cherry mixture stand 15 minutes.

Line 9-inch pie plate with pastry; fill with cherry mixture. Sprinkle with nutmeg. Dot with butter. Cover with top crust, cutting slits for steam to escape. Or, cut top crust into strips for lattice top and cherry leaf cutouts.

Bake in preheated 375°F oven about 1 hour or until crust is golden brown and filling is bubbly. If necessary, cover edge of crust with foil to prevent overbrowning.

Makes 8 servings

Note: Two (16-ounce) cans unsweetened tart cherries, well drained, can be substituted for frozen tart cherries. Dried cherries are available at gourmet and specialty food stores and at selected supermarkets.

Favorite recipe from **Cherry Marketing Institute**

Very Cherry Pie

White Chocolate Cranberry Tart

1 refrigerated pie crust (half of 15-ounce package)

1 cup sugar

2 eggs

¼ cup butter, melted

2 teaspoons vanilla

½ cup all-purpose flour

1 package (6 ounces) white chocolate baking bar, chopped

½ cup chopped macadamia nuts, lightly toasted*

½ cup dried cranberries, coarsely chopped

Toast chopped macadamia nuts in hot skillet about 3 minutes or until fragrant.

1. Preheat oven to 350°F. Line 9-inch tart pan with removable bottom or pie pan with pie crust (refrigerate or freeze other crust for another use).

2. Combine sugar, eggs, butter and vanilla in large bowl; mix well. Stir in flour until well blended. Add white chocolate, nuts and cranberries.

3. Pour filling into unbaked crust. Bake 50 to 55 minutes or until top of tart is crusty and deep golden brown and knife inserted in center comes out clean.

4. Cool completely on wire rack. Cover and store at room temperature until serving time. *Makes 8 servings*

Serving Suggestion: Top each serving with a dollop of whipped cream flavored with ground cinnamon, a favorite liqueur and grated orange peel.

White Chocolate
Cranberry Tart

Chocolate Fudge Pie

¼ CRISCO® Stick or ¼ cup CRISCO® all-vegetable
   shortening
1 bar (4 ounces) sweet baking chocolate
1 can (14 ounces) sweetened condensed milk
½ cup all-purpose flour
2 eggs, beaten
1 teaspoon vanilla
¼ teaspoon salt
1 cup flaked coconut
1 cup chopped pecans
1 unbaked Classic Crisco® Single Crust (recipe
   follows)
Unsweetened whipped cream or ice cream

1. Heat oven to 350°F.

2. Melt shortening and chocolate in heavy saucepan over
low heat. Remove from heat. Stir in sweetened condensed
milk, flour, eggs, vanilla and salt; mix well. Stir in coconut
and nuts. Pour into unbaked pie crust.

3. Bake at 350°F for 40 minutes or until toothpick
inserted in center comes out clean. Cool completely
on cooling rack.

4. Serve with unsweetened whipped cream or ice cream,
if desired. Refrigerate leftover pie.

Makes 1 (9-inch) pie (8 servings)

Prep Time: about 30 minutes
Bake Time: about 40 minutes

Classic Crisco® Single Crust

1⅓ cups all-purpose flour
½ teaspoon salt
½ CRISCO® Stick or ½ cup CRISCO® all-vegetable
    shortening
3 tablespoons cold water

1. Spoon flour into measuring cup and level. Combine flour and salt in medium bowl.

2. Cut in shortening using pastry blender or 2 knives until all flour is blended to form pea-size chunks.

3. Sprinkle with water, 1 tablespoon at a time. Toss lightly with fork until dough forms a ball.

4. Press dough between hands to form 5- to 6-inch "pancake." Flour rolling surface and rolling pin lightly. Roll dough into circle. Trim circle 1 inch larger than upside-down pie plate. Carefully remove trimmed dough. Set aside to reroll and use for pastry cutout garnish, if desired.

5. Fold dough into quarters. Unfold and press into pie plate. Fold edge under. Flute.

6. For recipes using a baked pie crust, heat oven to 425°F. Prick bottom and side thoroughly with fork (50 times) to prevent shrinkage. Bake at 425°F for 10 to 15 minutes or until lightly browned.

7. For recipes using an unbaked pie crust, follow directions given for that recipe.

Makes 1 (9-inch) single crust

Carnation® Key Lime Pie

1 *prepared* 9-inch (6 ounces) graham cracker
   crumb crust

1 can (14 ounces) NESTLÉ® CARNATION®
   Sweetened Condensed Milk

½ cup (about 3 medium limes) fresh lime juice

1 teaspoon grated lime peel

2 cups frozen whipped topping, thawed

   Lime peel twists or lime slices (optional)

BEAT sweetened condensed milk and lime juice in small
mixer bowl until combined; stir in lime peel. Pour into
crust; spread with whipped topping. Refrigerate for 2 hours
or until set. Garnish with lime peel twists.

Makes 8 servings

Carnation® Key Lime Pie

Blueberry Crumble Pie

1 (6-ounce) READY CRUST® Graham Cracker
   Pie Crust
1 egg yolk, beaten
1 (21-ounce) can blueberry pie filling
⅓ cup all-purpose flour
⅓ cup quick-cooking oats
¼ cup sugar
3 tablespoons margarine, melted

1. Preheat oven to 375°F. Brush bottom and sides of crust with egg yolk; bake on baking sheet 5 minutes or until light brown.

2. Pour blueberry pie filling into crust. Combine flour, oats and sugar in small bowl; mix in margarine. Spoon over pie filling.

3. Bake on baking sheet about 35 minutes or until filling is bubbly and topping is browned. Cool on wire rack.

Makes 8 servings

Prep Time: 15 minutes
Bake Time: 40 minutes

Blueberry Crumble Pie

Lemon Buttermilk Pie

1 (9-inch) unbaked pie crust*
1½ cups sugar
½ cup (1 stick) butter, softened
3 eggs
1 cup buttermilk
1 tablespoon cornstarch
1 tablespoon fresh lemon juice
⅛ teaspoon salt

*If using a commercial frozen pie crust, purchase a deep-dish crust and thaw before using.

Heat oven to 350°F. Prick crust all over with fork. Bake until light golden brown, about 8 minutes; cool on wire rack. *Reduce oven temperature to 325°F.* In large bowl, beat sugar and butter until creamy. Add eggs, one at a time, beating well after each addition. Add buttermilk, cornstarch, lemon juice and salt; mix well. Pour filling into crust. Bake 55 to 60 minutes or just until knife inserted near center comes out clean. Cool; cover and chill.   *Makes 8 servings*

Favorite recipe from **Southeast United Dairy Industry Association, Inc.**

Rustic Apple Croustade

1⅓ cups all-purpose flour

¼ teaspoon salt

2 tablespoons margarine or butter

2 tablespoons vegetable shortening

4 to 5 tablespoons ice water

⅓ cup packed light brown sugar

1 tablespoon cornstarch

1 teaspoon cinnamon, divided

3 large Jonathan or MacIntosh apples peeled,
cored and thinly sliced (4 cups)

1 egg white, beaten

1 tablespoon granulated sugar

1. Combine flour and salt in small bowl. Cut in margarine
and shortening with pastry blender or two knives until
mixture resembles coarse crumbs. Mix in ice water,
1 tablespoon at a time, until mixture comes together
and forms a soft dough. Wrap in plastic wrap; refrigerate
30 minutes.

2. Preheat oven to 375°F. Roll out pastry on floured
surface to ⅛-inch thickness. Cut into 12-inch circle.
Transfer pastry to nonstick jelly-roll pan.

3. Combine brown sugar, cornstarch and ¾ teaspoon
cinnamon in medium bowl; mix well. Add apples; toss
well. Spoon apple mixture into center of pastry, leaving
1½-inch border. Fold pastry over apples, folding edges in
gently and pressing down lightly. Brush egg white over
pastry. Combine remaining ¼ teaspoon cinnamon and
granulated sugar in small bowl; sprinkle evenly over tart.

4. Bake 35 to 40 minutes or until apples are tender and
crust is golden brown. Let stand 20 minutes before serving.
Cut into wedges.   *Makes 8 servings*

Decadent Brownie Pie

1 (9-inch) unbaked pastry shell

1 cup (6 ounces) semi-sweet chocolate chips

¼ cup (½ stick) butter or margarine

1 (14-ounce) can EAGLE® BRAND Sweetened
　Condensed Milk (NOT evaporated milk)

½ cup biscuit baking mix

2 eggs

1 teaspoon vanilla extract

1 cup chopped nuts

　Vanilla ice cream

1. Preheat oven to 375°F. Bake pastry shell 10 minutes; remove from oven. Reduce oven temperature to 325°F.

2. In small saucepan over low heat, melt chips with butter.

3. In large mixing bowl, beat chocolate mixture with Eagle Brand, biscuit mix, eggs and vanilla until smooth. Add nuts. Pour into baked pastry shell.

4. Bake 35 to 40 minutes or until center is set. Serve warm or at room temperature with ice cream. Refrigerate leftovers. *Makes 1 (9-inch) pie*

Prep Time: 25 minutes
Bake Time: 45 to 50 minutes

Grasshopper Mint Pie

1 (8-ounce) package cream cheese, softened
⅓ cup sugar
1 (8-ounce) tub frozen whipped topping, thawed
1 cup chopped KEEBLER® Fudge Shoppe®
    Grasshopper Cookies
3 drops green food coloring
1 (6-ounce) READY CRUST® Chocolate Pie Crust
   Additional KEEBLER® Fudge Shoppe®
    Grasshopper Cookies, halved, for garnish

1. Mix cream cheese and sugar with electric mixer until well blended. Fold in whipped topping, chopped cookies and green food coloring. Spoon into crust.

2. Refrigerate 3 hours or overnight.

3. Garnish with cookie halves. Refrigerate leftovers.

Makes 8 servings

Prep Time: 15 minutes
Chill Time: 3 hours

Grasshopper Mint Pie

Best-Ever Apple Pie

2⅓ cups all-purpose flour, divided

¾ cup plus 1 tablespoon sugar, divided

½ teaspoon baking powder

½ teaspoon salt

¾ cup plus 3 tablespoons cold unsalted butter, cut into small pieces, divided

4 to 5 tablespoons ice water

1 egg, separated

7 medium apples such as Jonathan or Granny Smith, peeled, cored and sliced

1 tablespoon lemon juice

1¼ teaspoons ground cinnamon

1 tablespoon sour cream

1. Combine 2 cups flour, 1 tablespoon sugar, baking powder and salt in large bowl until well blended. Cut in ¾ cup butter using pastry blender or 2 knives until mixture resembles coarse crumbs. Add water, 1 tablespoon at a time, to flour mixture. Toss with fork until mixture holds together. Form dough into 2 discs. Wrap discs in plastic wrap; refrigerate 30 minutes or until firm.

2. Working with 1 disc at a time, roll out dough on lightly floured surface with lightly floured rolling pin into 12-inch circle, ⅛ inch thick. Ease dough into 9-inch glass pie plate. *Do not stretch dough.* Trim dough leaving ½-inch overhang; brush with egg white. Set aside.

3. Preheat oven to 450°F.

continued on page 210

Best-Ever Apple Pie

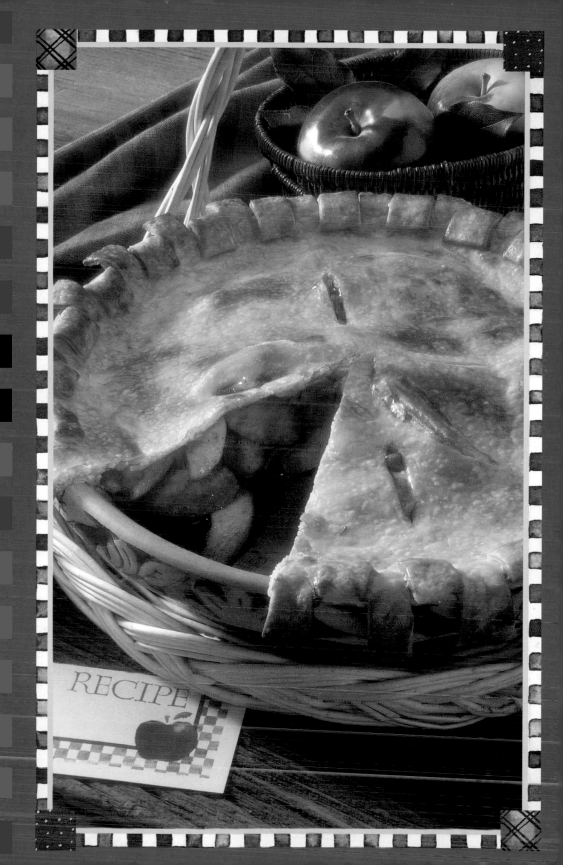

RECIPE

Best-Ever Apple Pie, *continued*

4. Place apple slices in large bowl; sprinkle with lemon juice. Combine remaining ⅓ cup flour, ¾ cup sugar and cinnamon in small bowl until well blended. Add to apple mixture; toss to coat apples evenly. Spoon filling into prepared pie crust; place remaining 3 tablespoons butter on top of filling.

5. Moisten edge of dough with water. Roll out remaining disc. Place onto filled pie. Trim dough leaving ½-inch overhang.

6. Flute edge. Cut slits in dough at ½-inch intervals around edge to form flaps. Press 1 flap in toward center of pie and the next out toward rim of pie plate. Continue around edge. Cut 4 small slits in top of dough to allow steam to escape.

7. Combine egg yolk and sour cream in small bowl until well blended. Cover; refrigerate until ready to use.

8. Bake 10 minutes; *reduce oven temperature to 375°F.* Bake 35 minutes. Brush egg yolk mixture evenly on pie crust with pastry brush. Bake 20 to 25 minutes or until crust is deep golden brown. Cool completely on wire rack. Store loosely covered at room temperature 1 day or refrigerate up to 4 days.   *Makes one (9-inch) pie*

S'more Pie

1 (12-ounce) chocolate candy bar, broken into pieces
30 regular marshmallows
¾ cup milk
2½ cups whipped cream, divided
1 (6-ounce) jar hot fudge topping, warmed
1 (9-ounce) READY CRUST® 2 Extra Servings
  Graham Cracker Pie Crust
Chocolate syrup, for garnish

1. Place chocolate bar, marshmallows and milk in medium saucepan. Cook over low heat, stirring constantly, until marshmallows and chocolate are melted. Cool to room temperature.

2. Fold 1½ cups whipped cream into chocolate mixture. Spread thin layer of warm hot fudge over bottom of crust. Gently spoon chocolate mixture into crust. Top with remaining 1 cup whipped cream and garnish with chocolate syrup.

3. Refrigerate 3 hours or until set. Refrigerate leftovers.

Makes 8 servings

Variation: Use a chocolate almond or chocolate peanut candy bar in place of a plain chocolate bar.

Prep Time: 15 minutes
Chill Time: 3 hours

Peanut Butter Pie

Chocolate Crunch Crust (recipe follows)
1 (8-ounce) package cream cheese, softened
1 (14-ounce) can EAGLE® BRAND Sweetened
    Condensed Milk (NOT evaporated milk)
¾ cup creamy peanut butter
2 tablespoons lemon juice from concentrate
1 teaspoon vanilla extract
1 cup whipping cream, whipped *or* 1 (4-ounce)
    container frozen non-dairy whipped topping,
    thawed
Chocolate fudge ice cream topping

1. Prepare Chocolate Crunch Crust.

2. In large mixing bowl, beat cream cheese until fluffy.
Gradually beat in Eagle Brand and peanut butter until
smooth. Stir in lemon juice and vanilla. Fold in whipped
cream.

3. Spread Eagle Brand mixture in crust. Drizzle topping
over pie. Refrigerate 4 to 5 hours or until firm. Refrigerate
leftovers. *Makes one 9-inch pie*

Chocolate Crunch Crust: In heavy saucepan over low
heat, melt ⅓ cup butter or margarine and 1 (6-ounce)
package semi-sweet chocolate chips. Remove from heat;
gently stir in 2½ cups oven-toasted rice cereal until
completely coated. Press on bottom and up side to rim
of buttered 9-inch pie plate. Chill 30 minutes.

Peanut Butter Pie

Nestlé® Toll House® Chocolate Chip Pie

1 *unbaked* 9-inch (4-cup volume) deep-dish pie shell*

2 large eggs

½ cup all-purpose flour

½ cup granulated sugar

½ cup packed brown sugar

¾ cup (1½ sticks) butter, softened

1 cup (6 ounces) NESTLÉ® TOLL HOUSE® Semi-Sweet Chocolate Morsels

1 cup chopped nuts

Sweetened whipped cream or ice cream (optional)

*If using frozen pie shell, use deep-dish style, thawed completely. Bake on baking sheet; increase baking time slightly.

PREHEAT oven to 325°F.

BEAT eggs in large mixer bowl on high speed until foamy. Beat in flour, granulated sugar and brown sugar. Beat in butter. Stir in morsels and nuts. Spoon into pie shell.

BAKE for 55 to 60 minutes or until knife inserted halfway between outside edge and center comes out clean. Cool on wire rack. Serve warm with whipped cream.

Makes 8 servings

Nestlé® Toll House® Chocolate Chip Pie

Perfect Pies

Hershey's Cocoa Cream Pie

1 baked 9-inch pie crust *or* graham cracker crumb
   crust, cooled
1¼ cups sugar
  ½ cup HERSHEY'S Cocoa
  ⅓ cup cornstarch
  ¼ teaspoon salt
  3 cups milk
  3 tablespoons butter or margarine
1½ teaspoons vanilla extract
   Sweetened whipped cream

1. Prepare crust; cool.

2. Stir together sugar, cocoa, cornstarch and salt in medium saucepan. Gradually add milk, stirring until smooth. Cook over medium heat, stirring constantly, until mixture comes to a boil; boil 1 minute.

3. Remove from heat; stir in butter and vanilla. Pour into prepared crust. Press plastic wrap directly onto surface. Cool to room temperature. Refrigerate 6 to 8 hours. Serve with sweetened whipped cream. Garnish as desired. Cover; refrigerate leftover pie.

Makes 6 to 8 servings

Hershey's Cocoa Cream Pie

Acknowledgments

The publisher would like to thank the companies and organizations listed below for the use of their recipes and photographs in this publication.

Cherry Marketing Institute

ConAgra Foods®

Duncan Hines® and Moist Deluxe® are registered trademarks of Aurora Foods Inc.

Eagle® Brand

Egg Beaters®

Grandma's® is a registered trademark of Mott's, Inc.

Hershey Foods Corporation

Keebler® Company

® Mars, Incorporated 2003

McIlhenny Company (TABASCO® brand Pepper Sauce)

Mott's® is a registered trademark of Mott's, Inc.

National Honey Board

Nestlé USA

The Quaker® Oatmeal Kitchens

Reynolds Consumer Products, A Business of Alcoa Inc.

The J.M. Smucker Company

Southeast United Dairy Industry Association, Inc.

Unilever Bestfoods North America

Index

METRIC CONVERSION CHART

VOLUME MEASUREMENTS (dry)

1/8 teaspoon = 0.5 mL
1/4 teaspoon = 1 mL
1/2 teaspoon = 2 mL
3/4 teaspoon = 4 mL
1 teaspoon = 5 mL
1 tablespoon = 15 mL
2 tablespoons = 30 mL
1/4 cup = 60 mL
1/3 cup = 75 mL
1/2 cup = 125 mL
2/3 cup = 150 mL
3/4 cup = 175 mL
1 cup = 250 mL
2 cups = 1 pint = 500 mL
3 cups = 750 mL
4 cups = 1 quart = 1 L

VOLUME MEASUREMENTS (fluid)

1 fluid ounce (2 tablespoons) = 30 mL
4 fluid ounces (1/2 cup) = 125 mL
8 fluid ounces (1 cup) = 250 mL
12 fluid ounces (1 1/2 cups) = 375 mL
16 fluid ounces (2 cups) = 500 mL

WEIGHTS (mass)

1/2 ounce = 15 g
1 ounce = 30 g
3 ounces = 90 g
4 ounces = 120 g
8 ounces = 225 g
10 ounces = 285 g
12 ounces = 360 g
16 ounces = 1 pound = 450 g

DIMENSIONS

1/16 inch = 2 mm
1/8 inch = 3 mm
1/4 inch = 6 mm
1/2 inch = 1.5 cm
3/4 inch = 2 cm
1 inch = 2.5 cm

OVEN TEMPERATURES

250°F = 120°C
275°F = 140°C
300°F = 150°C
325°F = 160°C
350°F = 180°C
375°F = 190°C
400°F = 200°C
425°F = 220°C
450°F = 230°C

BAKING PAN SIZES

Utensil	Size in Inches/Quarts	Metric Volume	Size in Centimeters
Baking or	8×8×2	2 L	20×20×5
Cake Pan	9×9×2	2.5 L	23×23×5
(square or	12×8×2	3 L	30×20×5
rectangular)	13×9×2	3.5 L	33×23×5
Loaf Pan	8×4×3	1.5 L	20×10×7
	9×5×3	2 L	23×13×7
Round Layer	8×1½	1.2 L	20×4
Cake Pan	9×1½	1.5 L	23×4
Pie Plate	8×1¼	750 mL	20×3
	9×1¼	1 L	23×3
Baking Dish	1 quart	1 L	—
or Casserole	1½ quart	1.5 L	—
	2 quart	2 L	—